MARTYN WAKELIN

Discovering English Dialects

Fourth edition, revised by
Professor J. D. A. Widdowson

Shrewsbury College of Arts & Technology

SHIRE PUBLICATIONS LTD

Published in 1994 by Shire Publications Ltd, Cromwell House, Church Street, Princes Risborough, Buckinghamshire HP27 9AJ, UK.

Printed in Great Britain by CIT Printing Services, Press Buildings, Merlins Bridge, Haverfordwest, Dyfed SA61 1XF.

ACKNOWLEDGEMENTS

Many people have generously contributed to the preparation of this book; thanks are especially due to the following: Mr J. Banks, Mr M. V. Barry, Dr P. Wright, Dr C. S. Upton; Professor P. Trudgill, Professor J. R. D. Milroy, Mrs B. Neale, Professor J. D. A. Widdowson, Mr R. Dobson, Mr G. Williams, Dr D. Parry, Miss R. Franklin, Mr K. G. Spencer, Mr P. M. Tilling, Miss N. Dawson, Mr O. Padel, Mr R. F. Wakelin.

I thank the following for permission to use previously published material: Mr S. F. Sanderson, for use of the *Survey of English Dialects* base map; the Board of Management of the Athlone Press for maps 1 and 3 (from M. F. Wakelin, *English Dialects*, second edition, 1977, pages 87 and 134, respectively) and map 4 (from M. F. Wakelin, editor, *Patterns in the Folk Speech of the British Isles*, 1972, page 186); the Secretary and Council of the Yorkshire Dialect Society for map 2 (F. Rohrer, *Transactions*, part 50 [1950], page 34), map 9 (E. Kolb, *Transactions*, part 65 [1965], page 12) and figure 4 (P. Wright, *Transactions*, part 66 [1966], page 42); Leicester University Press for map 5 (from M. F. Wakelin, *Language and History in Cornwall*, 1975, page 178); A. Brown & Sons for map 7 (from K. G. Spencer, *The Lapwing in Britain*, 1953, page 108); Oxford University Press for map 8 (from I. and P. Opie, *The Lore and Language of Schoolchildren*, 1959, page 177); André Deutsch for map 10 (from G. L. Brook, *English Dialects*, second edition 1965, page 62); J. M. Dent and Sons for figures 1 (from M. Hartley and J. Ingilby, *Life and Tradition in the Yorkshire Dales*, 1968, page 33) and 6 (from M. Hartley and J. Ingilby, *The Yorkshire Dales*, 1956, page 261); Faber & Faber for figure 2 (from G. Ewart Evans, *The Horse in the Furrow*, 1960, page 136; illustration by C. F. Tunnicliffe); the Federation of Old Cornwall Societies and the executor of the late Miss Mary Mills for figure 3 (from *Old Cornwall*, volume 8, number 3 [1974], page 141); Cambridge University Press for figure 5 (from A. Arber, *Herbals, their Origin and Evolution*, 1912, page 147).

Contents

ABBREVIATIONS

Corn.	Cornish
EDS	English Dialect Society
Fr	French
(M)Du	(Middle) Dutch
ME	Middle English
(M)LG	(Middle) Low German
OE	Old English
OF	Old French
ON	Old Norse
ONF	Old Northern French
RSE	Received Standard English
SED	*Survey of English Dialects*
•	Hypothetical, reconstructed form (i.e. unrecorded, but assumed to have once existed)

Single or double letters in bold type indicate *sounds*, not spellings.
Note especially the following:

a	as in *cat*
ah	as in *grass*
aw	as in *law*
ay	as in *late*
dh	as in *then*
é	as in Fr *té*
ea	as in *air* (approx.)
ee	as in *see*
i (long)	as in *fine*
ia	as in *ear* (approx.)
oo	as in *good* or *boot*
ooa	as in *doer* (approx.)
uh	as in *rust*
zh	as in *measure*

3

1. What are dialects?

We may usefully define *dialects* as sub-forms of languages which are, in general, mutually comprehensible, *languages* as forms which are not. The forms of speech local, say, to Wiltshire and North Yorkshire are dialect because, even though the local types of speech found in these counties are very different from each other, the people who use one can — in the main — be understood by people who use the other. This is not so with the forms of speech used in England and Germany, which are thus languages, not dialects. The Wiltshire man who says 'How be 'ee gwine ("going") on?' can be understood by the North Yorkshire man, with his 'Hoo ("how") is thou?' (however, compare, also from the north, 'What fettle?'!), but German 'Wie geht es Ihnen?' is only comprehensible to English people when they have learned German. Languages have progressed one stage further than dialects in their historical development.

Within any language there are likely to be different types of dialects. In English we need to note three in particular. These are:

(1) The old regional dialects of countryside and town

In their most complete form these are spoken best by older men and women who have lived in their own area all their lives, but middle-aged people and children frequently speak regional dialect to varying extents too. Often these latter use intermediate varieties, i.e. a basis of Standard English *influenced by* the dialect of their early years or their more recent surroundings, or a basis of dialect *influenced by* the Standard English they have adopted or are trying to adopt. For example, a native speaker of northern regional English may have become modified in the direction of Standard English so far as to lose some of his most distinctive 'native' sounds, such as **oo** in *mother, but,* replacing this by Standard English **uh.** Contrariwise, a person from the West Midlands who has long assumed a Standard English form of speech may be perfect in it except that he retains just one sound, e.g. the **g** sound at the end of words like *sing* and *hang.*

The dialects in their completest forms are best heard in countryside villages and hamlets and often appear in a broken-down form in the larger towns. Although there is bound to be a basis of, say, Yorkshire dialect in cities like Leeds, Bradford, Sheffield and York, over the years, perhaps mainly owing to influxes of industrial workers from all over Britain, such city dialects have become mixed not only with Standard English but also with other strains and thus differ to varying extents from the language of the surrounding countryside. (For example, it has already been shown that Norwich city dialect has been influenced by that of London.) Within a city, too, there may be several sub-

4

varieties, especially in the larger industrial complexes. Towns like Bradford and Corby are of special interest in this respect because of their history of mixed populations (West Indians in Bradford, Scots and Irish in Corby). It is in the cities that we can expect new syntheses of types of speech to emerge out of old varieties, and in this sense dialect is not dying at all, as it is sometimes said to be.

When discussing dialect, we shall find it necessary to distinguish various 'levels' — those of sounds or pronunciation, vocabulary and grammar — and examples of these in regional dialect are:

Sounds: The pronunciation of, e.g., *fish, sing, think, shall* in the south-west of England with initial **v, z, dh, zh**; the northern and midland use of an **oo** sound (as in Standard English *put*) in words like *mother, but*.

Vocabulary: *Gawp* 'stare', *nesh* 'soft', *bonny* 'pretty', *beck* 'stream' in parts of the north and midlands; *soak* 'make' (the tea) and *bladder* 'blister' in the south-west; *tundish* 'funnel', *pool* 'pond', *grains* 'dregs' in the west.

Grammar: The widespread use of the old pronouns *thou, thee, thy*, etc, and of *hisn, hern, ourn, yourn, theirn* 'his, hers, ours, yours, theirs'; the western forms of the verb *to be — I be, I bain't* ('I'm not'), etc.

Intonation. Intonation patterns (the different ways in which the voice rises and falls) in dialect have not yet been sufficiently studied, but we may draw attention to the very distinctive varieties of these to be found in the north (Tyne and Wear, etc), in East Anglia and in Cornwall. No doubt others also deserve attention.

Dialects outside England. This book is about regional dialect spoken in England; the English dialect of Wales, Scotland, Northern Ireland and the Isle of Man is not dealt with, because — apart from lack of space and the slightly complicating factor of the special histories of these areas — their dialects are not yet sufficiently documented to allow us to make general statements, and any treatment would inevitably have been scrappy and inconsistent. However, references are given to relevant sources of information, which are happily increasing, and it is hoped that the interested reader will consult these for himself.

(2) Social dialects

There is variation in speech between people of different classes as much as there is between people of different areas. At one end of this scale there is an ill-defined type of speech, a complex of numerous very similar varieties loosely held together in what we call Received Standard English (RSE), mainly in use among professional and educated classes (this includes affected varieties, e.g. the 'Oxford accent', which has nothing to do with Oxford itself); at the other end is a type of speech which usually still includes a substantial element of local dialect and perhaps a lot of slang. And in between these two we can hear the infinitely varied shades of speech from 'modified regional' at one end to 'modified RSE' at the other. This 'scale' of speech-types is likely to be best observed in large towns. We shall not be dealing very much with social variation in this book, but examples from either end of this scale are:

Sounds: Loss of **h** as in *'urt, 'ome, 'appy; a* (RSE *an*) before a vowel, as in *a egg, a 'andkerchief;* **n** (RSE **ng**) e.g. in *walking, going;* other more localised features, e.g. **a** (RSE **aw**) in *water* (i.e. *watter*); **ay** (RSE **ee**) in *tea* (i.e. *tay*).

Vocabulary: *Summat* (i.e. *somewhat;* RSE *something*); *as* and *what* (RSE *that* or *who*), as in 'the dog what I saw', 'someone as often goes there'; *learn* (RSE *teach*) — 'he learned me French', etc.

Grammar: Use of *our* (RSE *my*), *us* (RSE *me*) — 'give it us'; *ain't* (RSE *aren't*); *-s* ending in all parts of verbs — *I sings, we goes* (RSE has *-s* only after *he, she* or *it* or a singular subject); double negation — 'I ain't done nothing'.

And at all these levels, sounds, vocabulary and grammar, as has already been said, one end of the scale tends to retain local pronunciations, words and grammar, while RSE — essentially a non-local type of speech — loses them.

(3) Occupational dialects

These consist mainly of the specialised vocabularies used in different industries and occupations such as the aeroplane industry, the theatre, mining, barrel-making and so on. This sort of language, especially when it has no regional variation, is 'technical jargon' as well as dialect. Sometimes, however, there is a regional variation, as we can see from fishing and mining terms. Examples are:

Fishing: A short stick used in net-making is called a *kebble* or *kibble* (north-west coasts); a *shuttle* (mainly north-eastern); a *shale* (Humberside, East Anglia); a *lace* (north Devon, Cornwall, Dorset); a *scandle* (south Cornwall).

Mining: Poor coal is called *brockens* or *splints* (Tyne and Wear); *bags* or *muck* (South Yorkshire); *mothering* (Avon); *clod* (Gloucestershire); *rubbishy stuff* (Salop); *burgy* (Greater Manchester); *rubbish* (Cumbria).

Spoken and written forms

A careful distinction must be made between spoken and written forms of language, which are by no means the same. Speech is not based on writing (although attempts have been made to bring this about); otherwise we should have to pronounce, for example, the *gh* written in *knight* and the *w* written in *wrong*.

All the dialectal varieties we have mentioned are found in spoken form, which is what we shall be mainly concerned with in this book, but their occurrence in written form is less regular. Up to about AD 1450 all English, both spoken and written, was local, dialectal, but the written forms of these varieties gradually died out under the influence of Standard English, which began to rise to prominence from about the fourteenth century, although they may still be found in local documents (wills, accounts, etc) until much later. From about the sixteenth century onwards they also began to reappear in specially written 'dialect literature', which was intended to display the characteristics of the spoken dialects. By the eighteenth century this type of literature had become a flood, which continued into the nineteenth, and it is still written today. Of a rather different nature is the incorporation of dialect words and imitated pronunciations into novels and plays to give a dramatic effect, a practice which goes as far back as Chaucer and continues today.

Written social varieties of English are also sometimes used for special effect in literature. Charles Dickens, for example, includes imitation of the speech of widely differing classes of people in his portrayals of nineteenth-century life, and an eminent predecessor is William Shakespeare, some of whose characters' speech is of a lower-class stratum.

Occupational dialects appear in writing too, but usually only in special circumstances, when an author wants to create a realistic effect and needs to do so by the use of technical terms proper to the occupation he is writing about. Nautical language, for example, was used for literary effect in English as early as the fourteenth-century poem *Patience* (a verse homily on the life of Jonah) and as recently as the nineteenth-century American novel *Moby Dick*.

2. Some regional features

This chapter aims to draw attention to some of the more significant or interesting pronunciations, dialectal words and grammatical features which are to be found up and down England today, especially those which show definite regional *distributions*. The features mentioned, one must remember, are most frequently found in the speech of older people who have spoken local dialect since their early days, but many of them can also be heard from younger people.

The north

Pronunciation

England is divided by two very important boundaries in pronunciation: (a) dialect speakers of all ages, both young and old, in the northern part of England traditionally use a short **a** sound in words of the *grass, laugh, path,* and *branch, dance* classes, while in the south it is lengthened — most notably, speakers of RSE use a long **ah** sound; (b) the same (northern) speakers use an **oo** sound (as in RSE *put*) in words like *cup, butter, rough,* while southern speakers and speakers of RSE use a much more open sound (approaching **a** in the south-east), without the lips being rounded. Map 1 shows that the boundaries separating short **a** from the lengthened types and **oo** from southern **uh** are not as far north as is sometimes thought. Sometimes, in an attempt to come into line with RSE, younger dialect speakers produce hybrid forms, using a sound somewhere between **oo** and **uh** in *butter,* etc.

Within the northern area shown on the map we find another important boundary, dividing the north proper from the north midlands. This now runs — it has apparently been northward moving for some time — from the mouth of the river Humber, roughly along the Ouse and Wharfe valleys, and out of north Lancashire via the Lune and Ribble valleys, and represents the boundary which in Anglo-Saxon times, probably running much further to the south, divided Northumbria from Mercia; it is therefore an extremely ancient ethnic as well as linguistic boundary. It is characterised by a group of features of pronunciation only the most important of which can be given here. One of the most striking of these is the use of a long **oo** (as in RSE *boot, loose*) in words like *brown, cow, house* (thus *broon, coo, hoose*). In many places this is now tending to be replaced either by the RSE diphthong or an imitation of it.

A similar line marks off another set of distinctive pronunciations, namely those of sounds approaching **ia** or RSE *ear*, sometimes **i-oo**, in words of the *boot, fool, goose, spoon* class, and sounds approaching **ia** or **ea** (the sound in RSE *air*) in the *bone, loaf, road* class. In both of these classes attempts have been made over the years to conform more closely to the RSE pronunciation, and in the second class this has resulted in a very distinctive and persistent sound made with the lips rounded (as in the vowels of French *peu* or *feuille*) in Northumberland, Tyne and Wear and north Durham.

North of the Humber, and as far south as Lincolnshire, words in the *coal, coat, foal, hole* class (whose vowel is distinct historically from that in *bone, loaf, road,* etc) traditionally have a diphthong rather like that found in RSE *doer*, with the rounded sound (above) occurring again in Northumberland, Tyne and

Map 1. *Some* and *chaff* (after *SED:* the numbered localities are those of the *Survey*).

Key: —— General southern limit of **oo** in *some*.
     - - - General southern limit of a short vowel in *chaff*.

(Older northern and midland **oo** in *some*, etc, had probably become **uh** as early as the fifteenth century in some dialects, and has probably existed in RSE since *c.* 1550; dialectal lengthening of **a** before **f, s** and **th** in the south started in the seventeenth century, **ah** being adopted into RSE probably from south-eastern dialects sometime in the eighteenth.)

Wear and north Durham.

More or less the same boundary as these divides Northumbrian **ee, ia** in *eat, speak*, etc, from north-midland **ay.**

Map 2 shows how these old features of pronunciation cluster, marking off the area north of the Humber as a very distinctive northern dialect area.

Further north still Northumberland, Tyne and Wear and their environs are characterised by the retention of initial **h,** both in words like *hat, help, hurry* and in words like *what, when, which*. Although it is kept in RSE, most dialects have now lost initial **h** (although it is also found strongly in Somerset and East Anglia), and all the dialects *and* RSE have now lost the aspiration in words beginning with the letters *wh*. It is all the more singular, then, that this small area has retained both.

It also features a pronunciation first remarked upon by Daniel

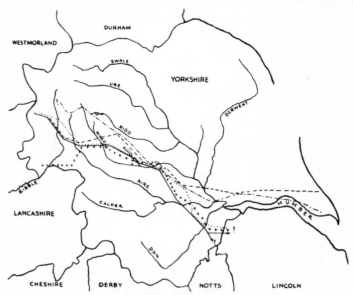

Map 2. Northern/north-midland boundaries.
   Key: southern limits of northern pronunciations:

··········	*coo* ('cow')
—·—·	*spian* ('spoon')
------	*bian* ('bone')
+++	*fooal* ('foal')
———	*iat* ('eat')

Defoe in his *Tour thro' the whole Island of Great Britain* (1724-7), namely the 'uvular' **r** (so called because made with the uvula at the back of the throat), sometimes known as the 'Northumbrian burr' or more popularly as the 'Geordie **r**' — what Defoe calls 'a hollow jarring in the throat'. Readers who wish to learn how to pronounce it should follow the instructions in Scott Dobson's excellent *Larn Yersel' Geordie* (Frank Graham, Newcastle, 1969)!

One or two features of pronunciation found in old, traditional dialect between the Humber and the small area we have just been considering remind us that this was an area of Scandinavian occupation. Although the region ultimately occupied by the medieval Norsemen extended very much further south than the river Humber (it comprised Anglo-Saxon Northumbria, East Anglia and Scandinavian Mercia), it is the north which now retains the most pervasive linguistic traces of their presence.

An example of possible Scandinavian influence on English pronunciation is the substitution of **sk** for **sh** in one or two words, e.g. *mask* 'mash' (i.e brew the tea) and (now obsolete) *skelf* 'shelf', *skift* 'shift', etc. The Scandinavians did not have the sound **sh** in their own dialects and substituted their nearest sound, which was **sk**.

A specially interesting word here is *pace-* (with loss of the **k**) or *paste-eggs*, the northern name for the eggs which children still dye and decorate at Easter time in Scotland, Ulster, the northern counties and north midlands (as well as on the Continent). The first part of this word is probably ON *páskar* 'Easter', which is in turn from Latin *pascha*. A traditional Northumbrian song, 'The Pitman's Courtship' (1818), runs:

> And to please the pit laddies at Easter
>
> A dishful of gilty paste eggs.

We do not hear of *pace-eggs* until 1579, according to the *OED*, but the custom is of ancient origin.

We also find substitution of **k** and **g** in words which in RSE have **ch** and **j**. This took place either by direct borrowing of the Scandinavian equivalent of the English word (e.g. *kirk* — ON *kirkja* — replaces *church* — OE *cirice*, whose *c*s were pronounced as **ch**) or by phonetic influence. Thus we find Scandinavian parallels to the RSE terms in *kirk* 'church', *kirn* 'churn', *birk* 'birch', for instance, all now somewhat obsolescent except in place-names (e.g. Kirkoswald, Bridekirk, Birkbeck); similarly *brig* 'bridge', *rig* 'ridge' (place-names: Brigstones, Brighouse, Brownriggs).

Vocabulary

Consideration of possible Scandinavian influence on northern sounds brings us to the question of northern vocabulary — although this does not imply that all or even most northern

Map 3. Scandinavian loan-words.

Key: ——— *steg*
.... *lea*
⊢——⊣ *ket*
– – – *stee*

vocabulary is derived from the medieval Norse dialects; much of it is as English in origin as is southern and midland vocabulary.

Many words, like *steg* 'gander' (ON *steggi, steggr*), *lea* 'scythe' (ON *lé*), *stee* 'ladder' (ON *stige*), *ket* 'rubbish' (ON *kjot*) are, as map 3 shows, spread over an area stretching diagonally right across northern England; to the north of this area, English words tend to predominate rather than Scandinavian ones, representing an area in which the Scandinavian presence was less strongly felt. Others — like *lop* 'flea' (probably ON *hloppa*), *lathe* 'barn' (ON *hlatha*), *sark* 'shirt' (ON *serkr*), *kay-fisted, -pawed* 'left-handed' (Danish *kei*) — occur now only in parts of this area, though they were probably once more widespread, while yet others, like *bairn* 'child' (perhaps ON *barn*, though maybe OE *bearn*), *beck* 'brook' (ON *bekkr*) and *neave* 'fist' (ON *hnefi*) are still widespread in parts outside this area. Some of these dialect words can also be found as elements in northern place-names (e.g. *lathe* in Silloth, *beck* in Beckwithshaw, Drybeck).

The Scandinavian element found in northern dialect is some indication of how much English, both dialectal and non-dialectal, owes to other languages. Such borrowing goes back to the earliest times, when the Anglo-Saxons took one or two words from their Celtic predecessors in England, words which are still current in dialect, like *brock* 'badger' (OE *broc*, from a Celtic source), now found only very occasionally though mainly in the north of England. The word *brat* 'apron', found in northern counties and occasionally in the north midlands, is probably from Old Irish *bratt* 'cloth', especially as a covering for the body, 'plaid, mantle, cloak', and is found in the north even as early as Old English times in the famous Northumbrian *Lindisfarne Gospels* (*c.* 950).

The foreign element in the vocabulary must not blind us to the richness of the native Anglo-Saxon contribution. Northern words like *wark* 'ache' (*teeth-wark, belly-wark;* OE *wærc*), *spelk* 'splinter' (OE *spelc*), *burn* 'stream' (OE *burna*), *ask, asker, askel, asgel, naskel*, etc 'newt' (OE *āthexe*), *nobutt*, i.e. 'nought but', 'only' (OE *nān + bē-ūtan*), *byre* (OE *bÿre*), *mistall* (OE *mēox* 'dung' + *stall*). *shippon* (OE *scypen*), all 'cow-house', *delve* (OE *delfan*) and *grave* (OE *grafan*), both 'dig' — all these are words firmly rooted in English soil from the beginning.

Much traditional vocabulary is thus still current in rural England, and in some industries the old words have apparently been pressed into new use: a Durham miner's snack is his *bait* and that of a Nottinghamshire miner his *snap* (from his *snap-bag*), both originally farmers' terms. The Sheffield steel industry uses words like *pens* for huge scrap-containers, and *strickle* as referring to the instrument used to smoothe the outside walls of a mould, perhaps transferred from its original usage referring to an instrument used for smoothing grain in a measure (OE *stricel*).

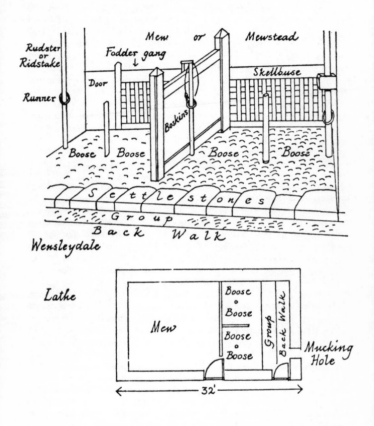

Fig. 1. The Wensleydale *lathe*. Note the terms *mew* and *mewstead* 'part of the barn where hay is kept' (OE *muga* + *stede*); *fodder gang* 'passage at head of cow-stall' (OE *fōdor* + *gang*); *boose* 'stall' (OE *·bōs*); *skell-buse* (or *-boose* 'partition'; cf. ON *skilja* 'to divide' + OE *·bōs*); *boskins* 'partitions' (OE *·bōs* + diminutive *-kin*); *rudster* and *ridstake* 'pole to which cattle are tied' (first part ? OE *wrǣd* 'band(age)'); *group* (or *groop* 'channel'; MDu *groepe*).

Grammar

Nouns. The older grammatical features of dialectal speech seem chiefly to be found in the south and west of England, but there are also some of interest in the north. In various parts of England nouns still have plurals formed in traditional dialect according to ancient methods, and in particular the so-called weak plurals still exist in some areas — i.e. forms like RSE *oxen*, derived from Anglo-Saxon times, with *-n* or *-en* added to the word to make the plural instead of *-s* or *-es*. *Shoon* 'shoes' is a northern example, stretching southwards, however, as far as Cheshire, Derbyshire and Staffordshire. *Een* 'eyes' likewise is still found as an old usage throughout the north and in some of the west-midland counties. Many others, recorded in the nineteenth century, *ashen* 'ashes', *peasen* 'peas', *toen* 'toes', etc, have disappeared.

Kine 'cows' is of special interest as a 'double plural' (i.e. a plural formed twice over, like children's *mices* or *mens*) made by adding the *-n* of the *oxen* type to the old plural form *kye*; it has been found in recent times only in Cumbria and North Yorkshire, but the more regular old plural form *kye* has been found in the northern counties and also in Cheshire and Staffordshire.

Pronouns. A feature of most older dialect speech (though to a lesser extent in the east midlands and south-east) is the use of *thou, thee, thy, thine* and *thyself* for 'you, your, yours' and 'yourself': northern 'dis th' remember . . .?', 'thoo seems it' ('it suits you'), 'I'm glad to see thee', 'I kenned (knew) thy voice', etc.

The forms of *-self* (in *myself, yourself*, etc) may appear in the singular as *sen, seln* and in the plural as *sen, seln* or *sens* in the north and midlands (*enjoying hissen, washing theirsens*, etc), all variant developments of ME *seluen;* and the simple personal pronoun *me, thee*, etc, is found for it in the north and west midlands and occasionally elsewhere — *wash me* 'wash myself', etc.

Demonstrative pronouns. In the north *yon, yond, yonder* are the most familiar demonstrative pronouns used to indicate an object 'over there', but *thir* 'these', *tho* 'those', *thon* 'that over there' and *thon ones* 'those over there' are perhaps less well known to southerners, likewise *thonder* 'yonder'. Perhaps these latter are combinations of *yon(d), yonder* and the pronouns which begin with *th*.

Prepositions and conjunctions. A dialect feature usually made much of is the use of the word *while* to mean 'until'. (A guide in York was recently heard to say to a group of foreigners 'All cross (the road) together and don't start to cross while I do'!) But this is not simply a northernism, although it is perhaps most common there; it is found also in the north midlands and east, and as far south as Berkshire. It was formerly much more widespread, being used, for example, by Shakespeare and Marlowe in this way.

Another item of interest here is *till* (ON *til*), which in north Cumbria (and occasionally elsewhere) can be used to mean 'to' ('till the doctor's', 'they gan ("go") till the kirk', 'quarter till twelve', etc).

Verbs. Apart from the fairly universal non-Standard *-s* ending in all present parts (*they keeps, we puts, I goes*, etc) the chief variations found in the north and in non-RSE speech generally are in the past tense and the past participle. In particular, we find numerous examples ending in *-ed* instead of having their usual form. *Knowed, growed, catched* and *seed* ('saw') are widespread, for example, and *comed* is also found in both north and south.

The verbs which in Anglo-Saxon times belonged to one particular conjugation show specially interesting archaic past tenses and past participles in present-day dialect: *give* has past tense singular *gav* in North Yorkshire, *get* has past participle *getten* and *gotten* in the north and north midlands; past tenses *spak* and *spok* are northern forms, as are also past participle forms *spok*, and *spak* (West Yorkshire), *spaken* (North Yorkshire).

Towns and cities

The area we have been discussing is mainly a rural one, apart from the great industrial complexes of Teesside and Tyneside. Towns like York, Richmond and Durham can be expected to share the major dialectal features of the surrounding countryside, except that these will perhaps be found in a less perfectly preserved state in the towns and there will be 'mixing' of types of speech. No doubt the locals will say they can distinguish the speech of a York man or a Richmond man or a Durham man from that of the countryside, but these distinctions are probably very local and minor ones to dialectologists, who are firstly concerned with mapping the most significant patterns.

The large cities, which have their own distinctive dialects, still await investigation, although an analysis has been made of pronunciation in Gateshead (W. Viereck, 1966), and a survey of Tyneside speech has been in progress from the University of Newcastle since 1963.

Meanwhile, on a lighter note, here, written in his own dialect, is what Mr J. Banks, a Sunderland man, sees as the difference between Sunderland and 'Geordie' (strictly the dialect of Tyneside). Sunderland people, he says, speak a dialect purely their own within a ten-mile radius:

> 'Dinnut think ave gorrout against being called a Geordie; av been proud ont in the past. But aa think wer should mak a distinction between the two, Geordies and Sunderlandonians.
> The mair north yer come, the rougher the speech

seems tu be. But that's understandable in my eyes.
We live a rougher sort of life. Take the shipyards and
the pit: if yu dinnut speak the twang they think the's
sommat wrang wi yer . . .' (*Sunderland Echo*, 15th
February 1975)

The midlands and East Anglia

Pronunciation

We have already considered 'northern' pronunciations which
extend into the midland area, namely the short **a** sound in *grass,*
etc, and short **oo** in *cup*, etc, so we can begin with the knowledge
that these same features are present in at least the northern half of
that area.

If we now consider the other sounds mentioned under 'The
north', we find that, in words like *cow, brown, house*, we usually
hear a diphthong rather like the RSE sound, but sometimes in the
north midlands and further south this has become almost or
completely a long pure sound (a monophthong — *caa, braan,
haas*), not infrequently like a long version of the **a** in RSE *cat,
glad*, not far removed from the Cockney pronunciation of *Ta-ar
Bridge*.

In words of the *boot, fool, goose, spoon* class, where the north
has the **ia** (etc) sound, South and West Yorkshire people
traditionally have a sound **oo-i**, which is found nowhere else in
England, and can refer to the *schooil* and the *mooin*, and can
threaten 'Ah'll sooin fettle thi' ('I'll soon fix you'); people in south
Lancashire, Greater Manchester, Merseyside, north-west
Derbyshire, Cheshire and Staffordshire, however, tend to
pronounce this as a long **oo** but with the tongue very far forward in
the mouth, giving an impression of the *u* in French *tu, lune;* this is
also the case in East Anglia and we shall meet it again in the
south-west.

The *bone, loaf, road* class continues in the north midlands with
a sound **ooa** rather like the diphthong in RSE *doer* — sometimes
being replaced by an **aw** sound in imitation of RSE so that, for
example, dialectal *coke* and RSE *cork* sound similar. In the rest of
the midlands one hears either a diphthong something like the RSE
one or a long pure vowel made with lips rounded, rather like
French *eau*. It is generally regarded as a special East Anglian
characteristic that this sound becomes long **oo** and certainly a very
close sound of this type may be heard there, but there is a more
general dialectal tendency in the midlands and south for this to
happen.

In the related group of words *coal, coat, hole* and others South
and West Yorkshire and central Lancashire uniquely have **oi** and
dialect speakers here can speak about a *coil-'oil* 'coal-hole' (even a

17

fish-'oil 'fish and chip shop') and a *fur coit* 'fur coat'. Perhaps the most evocative word to exemplify this sound, however, is *thoil,* i.e. *thole* (OE *tholian*) 'suffer, endure', etc, as in 'I couldn't thoil t'brass' ('I couldn't afford the money').

In words like *eat, meat, steal* (usually spelled with *ea,* but this does not include all words with this spelling), we shall often hear in traditional dialect a sound like RSE **ay** in Lancashire, Greater Manchester, Merseyside, South and West Yorkshire, Cheshire, Staffordshire, north Derbyshire and north Nottinghamshire (as well as in some other parts of the country). There is a traditional Yorkshire put-off: 'Them as *ayts* mooast puddin' 'll get mooast *mayt'* — 'Those who eat most (Yorkshire) pudding will get most meat'. All these, together with words like *sheep, green, weeds,* etc, have an **ee** sound in RSE, have a very complicated historical development and can be heard with various sounds in the dialects — if not with **ee,** then with **é** or the *'ear'* sound described above or the **ay** sound just mentioned.

In a west-midland area defined by an arc extending as far north as the south Cumbrian border, as far south as south-west Gloucestershire, and to the east enclosing a western strip of West Yorkshire, the western half of Derbyshire, all of Staffordshire and a western strip of Warwickshire (enclosing most of West Midlands) and north-west Gloucestershire, we can hear an **o** sound in words like *hand, gander, man,* where the vowel is followed by an **n.** This is a feature already evidenced in medieval manuscripts from the same area.

In the northern half of a similar area, extending a little further to the east but not so far north, we find another old pronunciation: in words like *hang, ring, tongue,* a final **g** is pronounced, where it is not pronounced in RSE. This is a very enduring feature, which one can hear not only from older people but from younger and more educated people.

A note on East Anglia. East Anglia shares many of the characteristic features of the midlands generally (see above), but stands out for its 'sing-song' intonation patterns, the closeness of the sounds in the *bone, loaf, road* class (*boon, loof, rood*) and *boot, fool, goose, spoon* class (see above), its retention of initial **h** and the frequency of the glottal stop ('a bi' o' bre' n bu'er'); among the older generation **v** may still be heard as **w** in, e.g., *viper, vinegar, victuals* (locally *wittles*) — but, again, this is a more widespread feature, preserved in Cockney, for example, up to the last century. These features, combined with a certain drawling articulation and a very rich dialect vocabulary, mark out the area as one of great interest and distinctiveness.

Vocabulary

A number of Scandinavian words penetrate midland areas, mostly in the east. *Stee* 'ladder', already mentioned, is an example of one that is recorded in much of West and South Yorkshire and Humberside; *stithy* 'anvil' (ON *stethi*) is found throughout Lincolnshire as well as the north; *slape* 'slippery' (ON *sleipr*) extends to north Derbyshire, north Nottinghamshire and most of Lincolnshire, and *bairn* and *beck* have also been mentioned. We can also note, among others, *lad* 'son' or 'boy', *lass* 'daughter' or 'girl', which are found in the north midlands as well as the north; *teem* 'pour' (ON *toema*) is now used in RSE only in the expression 'teeming with rain' but can be used in dialect with reference to pouring out tea and other things: a clear boundary across the country from north Cheshire to the Wash separates northern and midland *teem* from *pour*, although the latter is found further north, where it is clearly gaining ground over its rival. *Clip* 'shear' (ON *klippa*) is likewise current down to a boundary stretching from central Lancashire to south Norfolk.

A selection of other old and well-established dialect words might include those for:

Autumn: *Back-end* is still the usual dialect expression throughout the north and midlands (excepting Lincolnshire), contrasting with *fall* (*of the leaf* or *year*) in the dialect-speaking rest of the country.

Fig. 2. Mucking the land with a Suffolk *tumbrel*.

Brew (tea): The firmly entrenched midland word is *mash*, giving way to the (possibly) Scandinavian-influenced *mask* or *mast* in the far north.

Farmcart: Here a cluster of East Anglian words are of special interest — Essex *tumble*, Suffolk and south Norfolk (also Salop) *tumbrel* (see fig. 2), Norfolk *tumbler*, all probably of French origin.

Gutter (of a house): *Launder* is a French word too (OF *lavendier*), perhaps adopted from mining use, and now found only in North Yorkshire, Derbyshire and Cornwall. Northern *spout* (MDu *spouten*) gives way to *spouting* in the midlands (also found in the north), with the peripheral words *trough/troughing* (OE *trog*) found in East Anglia and on the Welsh and Yorkshire/Lancashire borders.

Hay-loft: *Tallet*, a Welsh border (and south-western) word in various forms (*tollet, tallent, tollant, tollart, talfat*), is derived from Welsh *taflawd* (ultimately from Latin) and may have spread from Wales by the agency of travelling people such as casual harvest labourers or drovers in the medieval period and subsequently.

Hedgehog: *Urchin* (ONF *herichon*) occurs in the west midlands and Welsh border area and also in a long diagonal sweep from the far north-west to central Lincolnshire. These two areas were probably once a united one, now deeply eroded by native and RSE *hedgehog*.

Path (through a field): *Pad*, a word of Low German or Dutch origin, is entrenched in the midlands and is a specially interesting word, being first heard of (*OED*) in 1567, and stated to be in origin a word of vagabonds' cant, which seemingly got into dialect as the ordinary word for 'path'.

Splinter: Various words, mainly of medieval German or Dutch origin, occupy the midlands — *speel* (of Scandinavian origin) is found in south Lincolnshire (as well as in parts of the north), with *spile* (MDu, MLG *spille*, etc) in Greater Manchester and Merseyside and *spill* (of a similar origin) in a small central Welsh border area; *splint* (MDu *splinte*) holds the west midlands, *shiver* (early ME *scifer*) most of Lincolnshire and Norfolk, *sliver* (OE *·slīfan + -er*) Suffolk, Essex and East Sussex, and RSE *splinter* (MDu *splinter*) the larger central and south-western areas of the country. *Speel* and *spill* are clearly related to the northern expressions *spelk* (OE *spelc*), *spell* and *spoal* (? ON *spolr*).

Grammar

The midlands have numerous grammatical characteristics different from both RSE and other forms of dialect.

Nouns with *-n* or *-en* endings are found occasionally: *flen* 'fleas' was recently recorded from Salop, Hereford and Worcester, and sometimes appears as *flens* in these counties. *Housen* 'houses', once apparently general in England except in the north, has been recently found among older people in two areas — one in Essex and East Anglia, and one in the west stretching from Hereford and Worcester through Gloucestershire to Oxfordshire and Berkshire, with occasional outliers.

Children is of special interest: the 'correct' form (historically speaking) is actually *childer,* which has developed quite regularly from ME *childre,* but an -*n* ending was added to some forms giving us present-day RSE *children. Childer* is, however, retained in dialect in the north midlands and occasionally in the south.

Map 4. Dialectal forms of *she* (after *SED*).

Pronouns. *Thou, thee, thy, thine* and *thyself* are used, though not in the eastern part of the area: except in the north of England, the forms *hisn, hern, ourn, yourn, theirn* are also widespread. The forms of the pronoun *she* (map 4), however, should be particularly noted: directly related to *she* itself is *shoo,* confined fairly closely to South and West Yorkshire. This may perhaps be a 'blend' or hybrid form of *she* and north-west midland *hoo* (OE *hēo*); such hybrids tend to arise when an area of one form abuts on to an area of another. Finally, *her* is characteristic of the central and southern west midlands and the south-western peninsula (except for west Cornwall).

In the old area of the West Riding of Yorkshire *us* can be heard for 'our' ('one on uz own', etc), and also in east Cheshire, north Derbyshire and north Staffordshire, and *we* 'our' has also been recorded in south Staffordshire. The use of these personal pronouns in possessive situations was once very much more common in dialect, and one could apparently use *we, us, thee, ye, you* and *he* for 'our', 'thine', 'your' and 'his' in different parts of England.

The pronoun *its* did not exist in medieval English and was, so to speak, invented — apparently in the south of England — towards the end of the sixteenth century, supplanting earlier and especially west-midland *hit* or *it.* (Shakespeare's Fool in *King Lear* says: 'For, you know, Nuncle/The hedge-sparrow fed the cuckoo so long/ That it had it head bit off by it young.') In the north midlands this old form *hit,* or *it* as it is now, is still used, i.e. in Lancashire, Greater Manchester, South and West Yorkshire, Humberside, north Derbyshire, east Cheshire, north Staffordshire and north Lincolnshire.

In addition to expressions like *wash me* 'wash myself', northern, midland and other dialects also use a pronoun where it is unnecessary in RSE — *sit thysen down, lie yourself down,* and even (in Lancashire and Derbyshire) *play them, play themselves.*

Conjunctions and prepositions of interest in the midlands include, as above, the well-known use of *while* for 'till' and that of *without* for 'unless' (throughout the west midlands and in Yorkshire, Humberside, central Lancashire, north Lincolnshire and north-east Leicestershire and also in some scattered southern areas).

Verbs. The present plural ending of verbs used to end in *-ath* or *-eth* in earlier times but has disappeared in modern RSE — *we come, you see, they have,* etc. A small area of the west midlands (mainly Derbyshire, Cheshire and Staffordshire), however, adds the ending *-n* or *-en* — already present in medieval times in this area — *we putten* 'we put', *han you . . . ?* 'have you . . . ?', etc. The strange-sounding *I bin* 'I am' — i.e. the usual western dialect form *I be* plus *-n* ending (see map 5) — also occurs in Salop and its

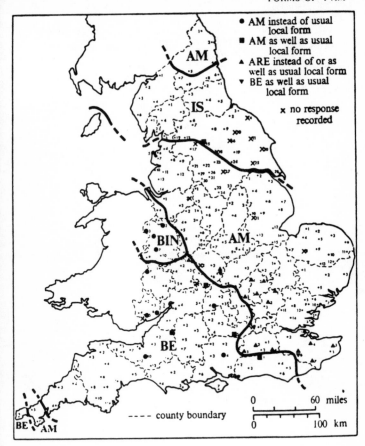

Map 5. Forms of *I am* (after *SED*). Note several important dialect areas: (1) a line roughly parallel with Watling Street divides *I am* from *I be;* (2) the Humber marks the southern limit of *I is* (ON *ek es*); (3) *I bin* (= *be* + *-n* ending) emerges as a sub-area of *I be;* (4) a small area of *I am* in west Cornwall represents the adoption of an early form of RSE here.

environs.

In the present participle (*I am going. they are sitting,* etc) an *a-* is prefixed in scattered places in the midlands, both east and west, as far north as Cheshire and as far west as Wiltshire and Gloucestershire (it is missing in Essex, Surrey, Kent, Sussex and Hampshire): 'I ain't a-going home yet', etc. This is a relic of the OE *on* which preceded the verbal noun.

Again, *-ed* forms are frequent in past tenses and past participles — *knowed, growed, weared,* etc, just as in the north. This is a common dialect feature, especially in these particular verbs.

And again, we find archaic forms in some verbs — past participles *getten* and *gotten* (still used in America) as in the north, biblical past tense *spake* (except in the eastern part of the midlands).

For *reach* the forms *roach* (past tense) and *roached* (past participle) are recorded in southern Northamptonshire, this verb having been re-formed on the model of *write-wrote, ride-rode,* etc.

Towns and cities

The mixed dialects of midland towns still await investigation. There are old glossaries of Sheffield dialect (EDS 57 and 62, 1888) and Leeds dialect (C. Clough Robinson, London — John Russell Smith — 1862), and people have written on the specialised dialects of cutlering and the steel industry (see *Transactions of the Yorkshire Dialect Society*). But published accounts of the dialects of Sheffield and Leeds as a whole — as well as those of Manchester, Liverpool, Nottingham, Leicester, Birmingham, Derby, Stafford, Peterborough, Northampton, Corby, Luton, Bedford — we still do not have. Dr Peter Wright, of the University of Salford, is engaged on city dialects and is expected to publish a book on these shortly. North Staffordshire speech has been studied in the University of Keele extra-mural department (see *Journal of the Lancashire Dialect Society,* 19, 1970).

The south and south-west

Pronunciation

Let us now look at the pronunciations we have traced down the country from the north, adding one or two others which are specially characteristic of the south of England.

The sound heard in *cow, brown, house* is, again, usually a diphthong, except in popular London speech, where once again we can hear that simple, pure sound without any glide — *kaa* 'cow', *braan* 'brown', *'aas* 'house' (not the sound in RSE *grass* or *car,* but further forward in the mouth).

A completely different and unique development has taken place in Devon, east Cornwall and west Somerset (see map 6), where the whole diphthong is pronounced with the lips rounded, the first part of it rather like the sound in French *peu*, the second like that in French *tu*. West Cornwall escapes this development because the type of English which came to be spoken there as Cornish was given up is thought to have been of a more 'standard' variety than that found in Devon and Somerset.

This also applies, in particular, to the very 'fronted' sound (as in French *tu* again) found in this area in *boot, food, moon, spoon, good, took, cook,* etc. We have already seen this 'fronting' (i.e. pronounced right at the front of the mouth) in west-midland counties and East Anglia, but it is more emphatic here in the south-west and quite unmistakable. Elsewhere in the south the sound is reasonably close to RSE. Attempts to find Celtic sources for these south-western phenomena (which mark off Devon, east Cornwall and west Somerset as a separate dialect area and are probably post-medieval developments) should be regarded with scepticism.

The *bone, loaf, road* and *coal, coat, hole* classes in the south

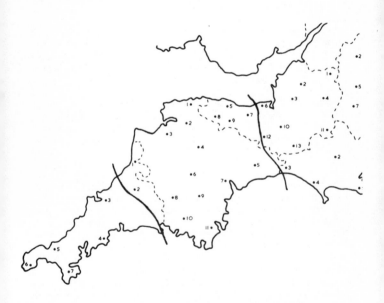

Map 6. The south-western 'rounded vowel' area (after **SED**).

remain recognisably close to RSE pronunciation — except that sometimes one can hear a long pure sound like that in French *eau* (or even closer) instead of the usual diphthong — and in the south-east, especially the London area, this becomes more like the sound heard in RSE *brown, cow, house.*

In words of the *eat, meat, steal* and *beat, leave, reach* classes (which differed from each other in their vowels in some Middle English dialects), older people in the south, as elsewhere, frequently use a pronunciation like RSE **ay** or French **é** — 'a good cup tay' ('a good cup of tea').

The vowel sound in *cat, lack, sad, stand,* etc, varies somewhat in the south from area to area. Over the greater part of England it is more or less like RSE **a,** but in two areas, namely parts of the south-west (the southern Welsh border and parts of Somerset and Avon) and the whole of the south-east, the sound is pronounced with the tongue slightly higher in the mouth, i.e. nearer to the RSE **e** position. In the London area and the Home Counties it does frequently attain to **e.**

In the south — including popular London speech — **o** before **f, s** and **th** is still an **aw** sound (*awff, crawss, clawth* 'off, cross, cloth'); this is now obsolete in RSE except in the speech of old-fashioned, conservative speakers.

A very important matter which arises in connection with southern and western dialects is that of the pronunciation of **r.** Not only are there more varieties than the one we hear in RSE, but **r** is also sometimes pronounced before consonants (e.g. in *cart, horse*) and at the end of words (e.g. in *hear, nor*) whereas in RSE it has been lost in those positions.

Firstly, then, the different varieties. 'Ordinary' **r** (as in *rabbit, mirage, hear it*) is found all over the main area of England. The other varieties are more peripheral. We have already noted the 'burr' in Northumberland and Tyne and Wear, and we occasionally find a 'trilled' or 'rolled' **r** in the north too. In the south-west (including Somerset, Wiltshire and Hampshire), **r** is 'reverted' or 'retroflex', i.e. it is pronounced with the tongue curled back further in the mouth than usual. In a small area of south Somerset this can be heard 'aspirated', i.e. as **hr.** In west Somerset and north-east Devon the **r** and a following **i** or **e** are sometimes reversed, so that one can hear *erd* (with the **r** pronounced) 'red', and even *herd* 'red', as well as the more familiar and more widespread (much of the south) *gurt* 'great', *purdy* 'pretty'.

Pronounced before consonants and at the ends of words, **r** is found — especially among older, more traditional, speakers — in a large south-western area stretching from East Sussex as far north as Cheshire and occurs again in Lancashire and the Pennine area. In Northumberland and Tyne and Wear the 'burr' can also be heard before consonants and at the ends of words.

We now have to consider one or two other consonant sounds in the south. Perhaps the best-known of these is the pronunciation at the beginning of words of **f, s, th** and **sh** as **v, z, dh** (as in RSE *then*) and **zh** (as in RSE *measure*), e.g. *varmer, zeed* ('saw'), *dhatch, zhilling*. This has long been familiar from stage dialect, but in reality it is now a very recessive feature, which, in medieval times widespread as far north as the Watling Street, is now found most consistently in Devon and the neighbouring counties, as well as Wiltshire and east Hampshire, although in some words (especially those beginning with **f**) occurring as far north as Gloucestershire and west Hereford and as far east as the western borders of Surrey and Hampshire. Outside this area examples are few and far between, though an odd one can apparently still be heard in East Sussex and the rural south-east. West Cornwall has fewer examples, once again because of its adoption not of south-western dialect but of a 'standard' type of English. When followed by **r** (e.g. in *three, through*), **th** in the south-west may be heard as **d,** so that we get *dree, drew,* etc. These sound-changes are evidenced historically in numerous place-names, such as Verwood (Dorset) 'fair wood', Venn (Cornwall) 'fenn', Vange (Essex) 'marshy district' (OE *fenn* + · *gē* 'district'), South Zeal (Devon) 'south hall' (OE *sele*), Zennor (Cornwall) 'St Senara', Druckham (Cornwall) — *Throcombe* in the fourteenth century.

In popular London pronunciation the simplification of **th** to f (*fank* 'thank', *moff* 'moth') and of **dh** to **v** (*ven* 'then', *gavver* 'gather') is well-known and indeed occurs further afield — in the Home Counties and even in the north. There is, however, an important group of words — *that, the, their, then, there, these, those,* etc — in which RSE **dh** is **d** in London dialect and the south-east, although younger people often produce a cross between **d** and **dh** instead of a fully formed **d.**

Finally, we must mention loss and addition of **w** and **y,** mainly in the south-west and west. At the beginning of words **w** may be lost before **oo** but added at the beginning of a word or inserted after a consonant before certain vowels. Thus, as far north as Salop and as far east as West Sussex (but not in west Devon and Cornwall) we can hear *'oman* 'woman' and *'ool* 'wool', but — more sporadically now — *wold* 'old', *bwoiling* 'boiling', *lwonely* 'lonely', *pwoison* 'poison', etc.

Loss of **y** in, e.g., *yeast, yes, yesterday, year* is much the same, except that we also find it lost in parts of eastern England (Lincolnshire, Suffolk). The addition of **y** is sporadically found — mainly in the south-west — in, e.g., *earn, earth* (thus *yearn, yearth*).

Vocabulary

We may now turn to examine a selection of southern dialect vocabulary.

Ant: *Emmet* — a word deriving from the same root as *ant* itself (OE *ǣmete*) — is the regular dialect word throughout the southern counties. A similar example is 'newt', which has a dialectal parallel *eft, evet, ewt, ebbet,* etc, throughout the southern counties, derived, like *newt,* from OE *efeta.*

Brew (tea): The two old southern dialect words are *wet* and *soak,* the latter only in Cornwall and west Devon, but the standard word *brew* is also found everywhere.

Farmyard: *Court* (a French word) or *back-court* is found in Wiltshire, Devon, east Cornwall and west Hampshire, alternating here with the native expression *barton* (OE *bere-tūn*).

Field: *Ground* (OE *grund*) survives in parts of the central south-west.

Mole: *Wont* (OE *wont*) occurs in the Welsh border counties and the south-west as far as west Hampshire.

Pigsty: West Somerset and east Devon have *lewze* (OE *hlōse*) for this item, but further down the south-western peninsula, in Cornwall, we find *pig's crow,* which, together with some more northerly counterparts, namely *pig-cree* and *pig-crew,* also *hen-cree, -crew, crewyard,* etc, derives ultimately from Celtic sources.

Retch: The south-western word for this idea is the expressive *urge* (perhaps a form of *retch*), but further north we find *heave* and *retch.* Interestingly *reave,* near the central Lancashire coast and in central Gloucestershire, may be a blend of *heave* and *retch.*

Scarecrow: Northern *flay-crow* (the first part perhaps from ON *fleyja* 'to scare, terrify'), midland *mawkin,* and various others give way in the south to *mommet* (OF *mahumet*), *gally-bagger* (OE *ā-gǣlwan* 'to alarm' + ?), and, in Cornwall, *bucca* (Corn. *bucca* 'hobgoblin', 'scarecrow').

One easily identifiable group of words in the south-west is those of Cornish origin. These, mainly the names of things, are chiefly restricted to the area west of Truro, where Cornish was last spoken, but some have been found further east. In addition to *pig's crow* and *bucca,* cited above, we may mention the following: *bannal* 'a broom' (Corn. *banal* 'broom flower or plant', 'besom'; cf. place-names Benallack, Carvannel, etc); *clunk* 'to swallow' and *clunker* 'windpipe' (probably Corn. *collenky* 'to swallow down'); *dram* 'swath' (Corn. *dram*); *fuggan* 'pastry dinner-cake' (Corn. *fūgen*); *gook* 'bonnet' (Corn. *cūgh* 'head-covering', etc, see fig. 3); *griglans* 'heather' (Corn. *grüglon;* cf. the place-name Gregland); *groushans* 'dregs' (Corn. *growjyon*); *hoggan* 'pastry-cake' (Corn. *hogen*); *kewny* 'rancid' (Corn. *kewnyek* 'mossy, mouldy, hoary'); *muryan* 'ant' (Corn. *muryon;* obscurely related to the second element in northern *pissy-moors, -moos, -mowers, -mires,* etc); *rab* 'gravel' (cf. Corn. *rabmen* 'granite gravel' and place-name Rabman Zawn); *scaw* 'elder-tree' (Corn. *scaw;* cf. place-names Trescowe, Nanscow, Nanscawn, etc); *stank* 'to walk, trample, step' (on, in) (Corn. *stankya*); *whidden* 'weakling' (of a litter of pigs; Corn. *gwyn*, later *gwidden* 'white').

Some of these Cornish 'loan-words' are not ultimately Cornish, but Latin, French or English, and have come into English *via* Cornish. From a very early period Cornish was susceptible to foreign influences to a remarkable degree, and its medieval and later literature is full of words and phrases from all three languages. Examples are:

Bulhorn 'snail' (Corn. *bulhorn*, a late Corn. word, adapted from an English dialectal nickname for the snail); *bussa* 'salting-trough', 'bread-bin' (probably ME *busse*, OF *buce*, *busse* 'barrel' and medieval Latin *bussa*); *croust* 'snack' (Corn. *crowst*, OF *crouste*, Latin *crusta*); *flam-new* 'brand-new' (*flam-* from Corn. *flam* 'flame', from Latin *flamma*); *geek* 'gape' (Corn. *gȳky* 'to

Fig. 3. Examples of the Cornish *gook*.

29

peep', perhaps from English *keek*); *hoggan* 'haw' (Corn. *hogan*, probably from OE *hagga* 'haw'); *peeth* 'well' (Corn. *pȳth*; cf. Latin *puteus*).

There may be, and there certainly once were, further Cornish words in the English dialect of west Cornwall, whether ultimately of Cornish or some other origin. But attempts to find Cornish words in Devon and elsewhere and attempts to find Celtic etymologies for everything in English dialect should be regarded with scepticism.

Grammar

Grammatically the southern area is one of conservatism (as compared with the north as an area of innovation), and it is here, especially in areas remote from London and the Home Counties, that we may expect to find the most ancient features of traditional English usage. Some of these, like south-western *utch* 'I' (ME *ich*), up to the last century found in Somerset, have now disappeared (*us* in south Somerset may, however, be a relic of this), but others — *thou, thee, thy*, etc — linger on.

Nouns. Having said this, it is odd that few traces of the old plural of nouns in -*n* or -*en* are to be found here, although the 'triple' plurals *hipsens* 'hips' (*hips* + -*en* + -*s*) and *hawsens* 'haws' (*haws* + -*en* + -*s*) have been found in south Oxfordshire and central Gloucestershire respectively. The regular old plural *chicken* (for RSE 'chickens', a double plural), OE *cicen*, plural *cicenu* (note, no -*s*), is found in the south-western counties and sporadically in the western and south-eastern counties (and, very sparingly, in Lancashire).

Pronouns. We have already mentioned the disappearance of *utch*; one ancient survival throughout the south-west, however, is *'n* 'him', 'it' — 'I seed ("saw") *'n*, 'put *'n* outside', etc — which is derived from the OE pronoun *hine* 'him' (pronounced hi-neh), lost to RSE, because replaced by the dative form *him* in early times.

In the south, more than anywhere else, we find the pronouns exchanging their functions, e.g. *she* (subject) being used for *her* (object) and *her* for *she*, but there usually seems to be a restriction on this process in that the objective form is used for the subject only when the pronoun is being used in unemphatic situations (e.g. *didn't her?* '... didn't she?'), and, contrariwise, the subject form is used only as the emphatic form of the object (e.g. *I told she*). In the south-west, then, we find *I* used for 'me', *we* for 'us' (this also embraces all the south except for Surrey, Kent and the south-east), *he* for 'him', *she* for 'her' (less common), and *they* for 'them'; contrariwise *us* for 'we' (spreading into the south midlands), *him* and *'n* for 'he', *them* for 'they' (spreading into the west midlands).

In east Cornwall the strange-sounding pronoun *mun* 'them' (*be mun . . . ?* 'are they . . . ?', etc) occurs — it was current in

Somerset, Devon and Cornwall in the nineteenth century; its origin and history are obscure.

Thou, thee, thy, etc, are, of course, used in the south (except in the eastern part), as is also *ye,* usually current as *'ee.*

Demonstrative pronouns. These show some interesting forms here, especially the well-known *thick* (the *th* pronounced as in RSE *this*), *thicky* 'this', *thuck, thucker* 'that' (all from ME *thilke*), and *theseum* 'these'. *They* ('those') — 'in they days', etc — is also in frequent use.

Adjectives. We have not so far had cause to mention adjectives, since in the north and midlands these are very much the same as in RSE. In the south, however, we meet an interesting deviation. In RSE many adjectives denoting material end in *-en,* e.g. *wooden, golden* (and cf. the archaic 'in the olden days'), and this is extended further in the south-west, so that a farmer shears his sheep 'down on the *boarden* floor' (of the barn), a child eats his sweets out of a *papern* bag, and cake that is not home-made is necessarily *boughten* cake.

Verbs. The *to* which occurs before a verb has a widespread dialect parallel form *for to* (as the song has it, 'I want for to go to Widecombe Fair'), and in the south the *to* often completely disappears, leaving us with, e.g., 'I came for see the doctor', 'you've got for know how to do it'.

One or two examples of the extremely ancient and rare third singular *-eth* ending remain in east Cornwall and south Devon. This derives from Old English but began to be supplanted by *-es* in Middle English, although the old *-eth* forms were retained as late as the seventeenth century, e.g. in the Authorised Version of the Bible (1611). The ending is rare now, but *her wear'th* 'she wears' and *her'th returned* 'she's returned' have been recorded in recent times in east Cornwall, and *dooth* 'does' (also *I'th seen*) from south Devon.

Sometimes the *-eth* ending was lost in Middle English *without* being replaced by *-es,* thus giving a form with no ending. Such forms are fairly frequent in the present-day southern dialects, especially in the south-west and East Anglia, where we can find, for example, *she wear, it hurt* (present tense).

The infinitive form (modern English *come, ride, see,* etc) of some verbs ended in *-ian* in Old English (*gaderian* 'gather', *nerian* 'save', etc), and there seems to be a relic of the *-i-* of this form left in some south-western verbs; thus, for example, (north Devon) 'There isn't many (who) can sheary ("shear") now'. The *-y* ending, however, is probably added to verbs indiscriminately now, as in the Cornish proverb 'They that can't schemy (i.e. use their brain) must lowster' (i.e. do labouring work).

In RSE *do* is only used with the infinitive in certain situations: questions — 'Do you see?', emphasis — 'I do want to', negation —

'I don't know'. But in the south-west it is often used with the infinitive in contexts such as 'I d'go every day', 'as far as I d'know', 'He d'come here on Tuesdays'. This occurs in an area round the river Severn comprising places in south-west Hereford, Gloucestershire and Avon, in another very small area in central and west Cornwall, and in a third, larger area comprising parts of Wiltshire, Dorset and environs. But these were all probably once part of a large connected area.

Again here the present participle is found prefixed by *a-*: 'There she was, *a-going* down the road . . .' Further, the past participle was sometimes prefixed by *ge-* in Old English (ME *y-*, *i-*), and traces of this too remain in the south-west as *a-* in, e.g., *a-found, a-put, a-done, a-broked* ('broken').

The *-ed* forms of past tenses and past participles continue in the south, e.g. *borned* 'born' (recorded from west Cornwall; = past participle *born* + *-ed* ending); *wored* 'worn' (south Somerset, Cornwall); *wored* 'wore' (west Somerset); *woreded* 'worn' (central Devon); *stoled* 'stole, stolen' (south-west); *doed* 'done' (south-west).

Strange and archaic forms in some of the verbs, due to past changes in the language, are again to be found in the south, e.g. *gov* 'gave, given' (recorded from west Cornwall), *sot* 'sat' (west Somerset, central and south Devon), *spok* 'spoken' (south-west), *spake* 'spoke' (north-west Surrey).

Towns and cities

In the south we do not find the large industrial towns of the midlands, but we do have to take into account the influence of popular London dialect, with its characteristic sounds: roughly **a** (*cab, matter*) tending towards **e; o** in *off, cough*, etc tending towards **aw; uh** (*butter, mother*) towards **a; ay** (*gate, change*) towards long **i** (RSE *fine*, etc); long **i** (*line, type*) towards **oi;** the sound in *no* towards that in *now;* **th** in *this, there*, etc becoming **d;** frequent use of the glottal stop (*bu'er, wa'er*); **l** becoming 'vocalised' to **oo** in, e.g., *bull, field* (roughly *boo, fiood*). Many of these are also characteristic of Cockney proper, from which, however, we may add **ow** becoming an **ah** type of sound (*tahn, 'ahs*), **f** for **th** in, e.g., *think, thirty*, and perhaps **aw** for **ah** in *heart, last*, etc.

First of all, as London has spread its suburbs further and further out into the countryside of the Home Counties, so its dialect has gone with it — with pre-war suburban settlers, wartime refugees and others who left London for what was then countryside and have stayed since. As this sprawl has eaten up the country villages, so its suburban tongue has gradually obliterated the old country speech in counties like Kent, Surrey and Sussex, once the homes of traditional English dialect as much as Devon and Yorkshire still are. And a contributory factor to this loss of dialect is no doubt the replacement of native villagers by commuters.

Furthermore, this popular London dialect has pushed its way to the south and east coasts and up as far as Norwich (which may account for Jonathan Mardle's judgement, in his *Broad Norfolk*, that Norwich 'has developed a slipshod urban argot that is different from, and inferior to, old-fashioned Norfolk . . . an adenoidal gabble, which schoolmasters justly deplore'!). The constant bombardment of the south-eastern holiday resorts by Londoners may be partly responsible for this, as may also commuting. But whatever the causes, the traditional features of many of these dialects (e.g. the 'retroflex' **r** formerly heard in words like *carter* and the **v, z,** etc, in words like *field* and *son*) have all but disappeared and are absent in the speech of younger people, except perhaps in the far reaches of the countryside. The old dialects of the south-east are thus undergoing a complete change.

3. Occupational and specialised vocabularies

The distinctive features of the special dialects of farmers, railway workers, fishermen, actors, civil servants and so on are found mainly in their vocabularies, although the members of these groups will also, in general, use the sounds and grammar of their own social class, and — if they have a regional dialect — also of their geographical region. (However, there are also special 'voices' associated with some professions — we can all recognise that of a sergeant major on parade, and sometimes, perhaps, a clergyman in his pulpit.) Here, then, we shall exemplify what makes, say, miners or steelworkers linguistically distinct as a group, namely the words they use in the industry or in contexts closely associated with it, and consider how these terms differ from place to place up and down the country in the same occupation. Naturally, we cannot give examples from every industry but shall deal with one or two of those which have been investigated.

Farming

Many farming words have already been mentioned within the regional plan we adopted, and here we can exemplify specialised aspects of farming by looking at one further group of words. This group relates to haymaking in the Yorkshire Dales, which is really three processes, mowing, haymaking proper and *leading*.

(1) Mowing machines were not introduced into the Dales until the second half of the nineteenth century, but hand-mowing with a *lea* (scythe) is only remembered by the very elderly now. Before

hay-time, mowers selected their own pole and the *lea* was then set up by the blacksmith, consisting of *shaft* (pole), blade, nibs (upper and lower), heel hoop, wedges and grass-nail. Attached to the top end of the *shaft* was a wooden *strickle* for whetting.

(2) Once scythed, the grass was submitted to a process of *strawing* or *shaking out*, turning, drying in small heaps called *foot-cocks*, larger ones called *jockeys* or even larger ones called *pikes. Strawing* by hand was the most approved way: up to about sixty years ago *straw-girls* or *straw-boys*, about four to one mower, followed the scythemen across the field and *strawed* the grass by bending low and tossing it alternately with each hand over the opposite shoulder. But the frequently employed Irishmen, using forks, could *straw* or *scale* two rows at a time of the hand-mown *swiaths* (swathes). When built, the haycocks were protected from the wind by a hay-rope thrown over them, made with the help of a *thraw-crook* or a rake.

(3) *Leading*, or carrying the dry hay to the *lathe* (barn), was done by *sweeping* it with a *hay-sweep* (a gate-like wooden frame) or piling it on to a sledge, pulled by a horse or perhaps two. When using a sledge, two men at each side gathered together *kemmings* ('combings' — i.e. armfuls) of hay with their rakes and placed them on in layers. The whole was then secured by a rope.

Loads were tipped off sideways; the *forker-up* then tossed the hay with a fork through a hole into the *mewstead* or *up on t'baulks* (loft over the cow-stalls) where it was spread evenly and trodden well down. Finally, *knag-* or *drag-rakes* were pulled by hand up and down the meadows to collect hay that had been missed.

Layers of hay cut with the hay-knife or hay-*spiad* (-spade) from the hay in the *mewstead* were called *desses* (*canches* in Swaledale).

Haymaking was an exhausting process and the workers no doubt richly deserved their break or *bait, drinking(s)*, or *ten-o-clocks*, and also the supper or *mell* which marked the end of this annual procedure.

The technical terms which have emerged here are local to one comparatively small region: farmers in Devon or Wiltshire would use a quite different set. Our next example shows how such technical terms vary from area to area round the country.

Fishing

Fishing is another traditional British occupation, but both this and mining are less stable than farming, and there has been (and still is) much movement of workers between areas. This results in the transference of words from one part of the country to another, and thus they become geographically widespread within the industries concerned.

Two surveys of fishing terms have been carried out, one by Dr Peter Wright, of the University of Salford (see the *Journal of the*

Lancashire Dialect Society 16-17, 1967-8), and one by Dr W. Elmer, of Basel, and the selection below is taken from these surveys.

The types of the old local boats — the number of which is now considerably diminished — provide a rich variety of local names: the widely distributed *smack* is an example of a term which still survives even though the type it once described has changed or disappeared; the south-western *gig,* on the other hand, illustrates how old names are transferred to new boats of different structure (they are now motor-powered). From the north-east coast come *cobles* (*yawls* on Holy Island), while in East Anglia we find *alongshore boats, crab-boats* and *toshers; beach-boats* and *luggers* are found in the south-east, and in Cornwall and Devon *crab-boats* and (again) *toshers;* the north-west has *nobbies* among others; *punts* are found in East Anglia, the south-east and the north-west.

The various parts of the boats also produce local terms. Here once again there are differences in structure: there are, for example, three types of fulcrum in the boats, namely *rowlocks,* turning on a pin (universal); *tholes* or *tholepins,* vertical wooden pegs between which the oar works (almost as widespread); and *oar-ports,* a Scandinavian feature now found only in the crabbers of Cromer, Sheringham and Mundesley, which consist of two to three holes in the top plank called *orruck-holes* (from ME *orloc,* which is also the basis of *rowlock*).

Crab and lobster pots are also of different types — three main ones are used around the English and Welsh coasts: the south and south-west is the home of the *Cornish pot;* on the east and south-east coasts are found the *creel* or *creeve;* the recently introduced *barrel* type or *Frenchman's pot* is apparently gaining ground along the south coast.

One can still see part-time fishermen shrimping with a *pushnet* and a shrimp-basket in shallow waters, and this basket may be known as a *bushel-* (north Norfolk), *butter-* (Sussex) or *keep-basket* (west Cornwall), a *creel* (east and north coasts), a *skep* (Suffolk), a *swill* (Lancashire), among others.

The fish themselves have a great variety of names. The starfish has so many local names that it is hard to select. *Five-finger(s)* is found everywhere except the far north, with variants *fivelegs, fivefeet, fivetoes* occurring much less regularly. *Thorns* is a north-eastern term, as is also *frawns; hornheads* is found in north Norfolk, *cross-fish, cross-ones* in Lancashire and Cheshire.

A glance at even this minute selection of words shows some differences in the distribution of items. Some are widely accepted all round the coasts, e.g. *rowlocks,* also *braiding* (OE *bregdan*) 'net-making, -mending', and are thus trade jargon rather than regional dialect. Others are restricted to specific areas, like (mainly) north-western *web* 'oar-blade' and a south-western group *nozzle, nozzling, orsle* 'snood' (the thin line by means of which the hook is attached to the main line in 'long-lining', a type of winter fishing). Finally, some occur at widely separated places, indicative of the fishermen's movement from one place to another, e.g. *beeting* (OE *bētan*) 'net-making, -mending', found in Cleveland, North Yorkshire and Humberside, East Anglia, Kent and Sussex and the far west of Cornwall; *black-jack* 'coal-fish', found on the north-east coast, Suffolk, Essex, Kent, south Devon, Swansea and Cumbria; *shuttle* 'short stick for braiding', found in a cluster of north-eastern localities and in isolated instances in north Norfolk and West Sussex.

Mining

In mining, as in fishing, there have been frequent and large-scale movements of workers from one place to another, e.g. the large migrations which recently took place from County Durham to the Yorkshire-Derbyshire-Nottinghamshire coalfield and from the Forest of Dean to South Wales. Presumably reflecting this mobility, the keynotes of a recent investigation, again by Dr Peter Wright, are, on the one hand, variety — variety of words for one single notion within a small area — and, on the other, the widespread distribution of some words. Taking the second aspect first, a miner's working-place, for example, is known as *stall* in several midland coalfields and also in Gloucestershire, a water channel as *garland* in both North Wales and Somerset. Examples of the first aspect are: for 'stint' (i.e. the amount of work allotted to one miner), *stint, pog* and *sneck* from pits in the old West Riding of Yorkshire within a ten-mile radius of each other; for 'stallman' at Warsop (Nottinghamshire), *chargeman, stallman* and *butty*. In the Somerset pit, vertical wooden props are apparently *posts* if under three feet, *timber* if longer; *uprights* was given by an informant's friend during the survey, and they appear in broader dialect as *stimples* — in other words, four terms for a single basic idea.

A further small selection of terms from coalfields in different counties from Dr Wright's survey might include:

Miner: *Miner* itself (perhaps mainly southern), *collier* (perhaps mainly northern), and *pitman* in places as far apart as Tyne and Wear and Kent.

Pit-head: Sometimes *pit-top* is used for this, and we also find *bank* in Tyne and Wear, in South Yorkshire *pit-top* together with older *pit-bank* and technical *heap-stead*, and in Greater Manchester *heap-stead* and more modern *pit-brow*.

Haulage road: *Jig* (Salop), *rope road* (Nottinghamshire), *ginny* (South Yorkshire and Gloucestershire), *incline* (Somerset), *steep* (Kent), *spinney-brow* (Greater Manchester).

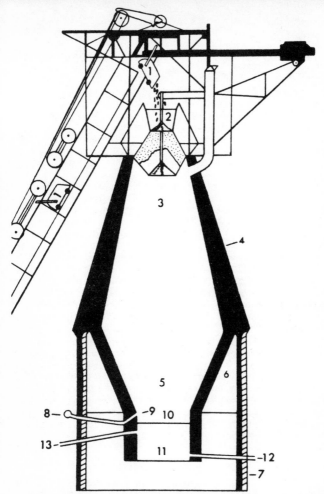

Fig. 4. A further example of industrial vocabulary: diagram of a Sheffield blast-furnace with parts labelled. 1 *skip* (small wheeled container to charge the furnace); 2 *hopper* (container for receiving the ore and passing it into the furnace); 3 *throat;* 4 *stack* ('chimney'); 5 *belly* (widest part of stack); 6 *bosh* (container round the belly); 7 *mantle* (to support the stack); 8 *bustle pipe* (distributing hot blast); 9 *tuyeres* (nozzles through which the air enters the furnace); 10 *hearth;* 11 *bottom;* 12 *slag-hole* or *slag-notch* (the place where the cinders, etc, come out); 13 *tap-hole* (small opening through which the metal is run out).

Deputy: In addition to *deputy* itself, there are *examiner* (Somerset) and *doggy* (Greater Manchester, South Yorkshire).

Depression in roof: *Slip* (West Yorkshire, Nottinghamshire), *pot-hole* (South Yorkshire, Nottinghamshire, Greater Manchester), *stone* (Tyne and Wear), *bad stone* (north Cumbria), *bad hole* (Nottinghamshire), *bad ground* (Salop), *bell* and *welver* (Gloucestershire), *bell-mould* (Somerset).

Brake on a tub: *Cow* (Tyne and Wear), *lashing-chain, clam-key* and *drag* (South Yorkshire), *clivvy* (Nottinghamshire), *lounge* (Somerset), *sprag* (Gloucestershire), *locker* (Salop), *coupling* (Greater Manchester).

An investigation of north Staffordshire terms meaning 'late for work' has been directed by Mr J. Levitt (see *Journal of the Lancashire Dialect Society* 19, 1970), the most common word being *franked*, used throughout the area, and the second most common *buzzed* (with obvious allusion to the buzzer being sounded), also in use in Cannock (south Staffordshire). To the north of Stoke-on-Trent, in Biddulph, Norton and Smallthorne, the word *sornet* (? = 'sounded') is in use; and in the village of Audley and in Tunstall, *in Dicky's meadow* has been reported ('Wey shall av't hurry up, or wey sal bey in Dicky's meadow', i.e. in 'queer street', i.e. late).

Overlain 'overslept' is the main reason for being late at work, but at Froghall in the Churnet valley the word *flung* occurs, which means 'made late': 'I was flung this morning and got franked'.

This scrutiny of a small area suggests that a nationwide survey of such terms would be exceptionally interesting.

A wealth of vocabulary clearly remains to be harvested not only from heavy industry but from such country crafts as charcoal-burning, basket-, hurdle-, hoop- and rake-making, coopering, smithing, thatching, brick-making, potting, wool-working, tanning, boot-making, and many more too numerous to mention (see especially the books by Jenkins and Hartley under Further Reading).

Bird and plant names

Local names for birds, animals and plants are a far cry from industrial language. Some domestic animal names have already

Map 7. Local names of the lapwing in Britain. Key: 1 *teeick* or *teeack;* 2 *teuchet;* 3 *peewit* and *peesweep;* 4 *tewit;* 5 *teäfit* or *teufit;* 6 *peewit* (a) *peewit* plus *plover,* (b) *peewit* plus *plover,* also *piewipe,* (c) *peewit* plus *plover,* also *horniwink;* 7 *green plover* (the broken line indicates that this can also be heard in south-west Scotland and certain of the Isles); •*lapwing* used popularly.

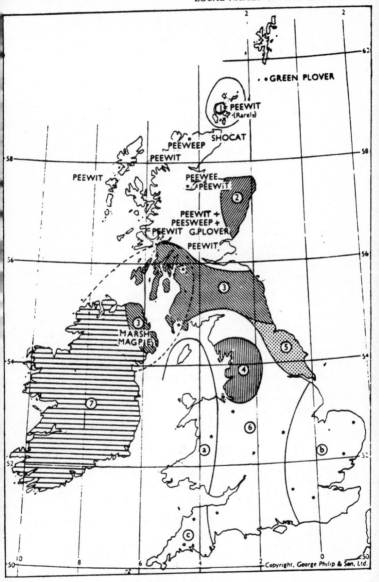

been mentioned. For birds, we cannot do better than look at the map (map 7) of the lapwing's local names. This is one of the few pieces of research done on bird-names, and its author, Mr K. G. Spencer, also carried out a survey of Lancashire bird-names (see *Journal of the Lancashire Dialect Society* 14, 1965); this, in turn, was inspired by Mr J. C. Maycock's similar survey in Yorkshire (see *Transactions of the Yorkshire Dialect Society*, Parts 53, 54, 56, 1953-6). A nationwide survey of bird-names is urgently needed.

We take as an illuminating example of local variation in plant-names the old titles of the bindweed. Apart from *bindweed* and *bind*, which are of general occurrence, *convulvulus* occupies much of the north (down to North Yorkshire) and a long strip of country comprising west Lancashire and Merseyside, most of Cheshire and Salop, while *ground-ivy* occupies another well-defined area in the south-west consisting of Cornwall and Devon except for the south-east. Throughout the rest of the country, names ending in *-bind* or *-wind* (*-vine* in west Suffolk, Cambridgeshire, Bedfordshire and Hertfordshire) predominate: *with(y)-wind* and *bith(y)-, bes-, beth-, beddy-, betty-wind* in most of the south, also *bell-wind* and *willy-wind*, a very large east-midland area of *cornbind*, stretching from Humberside and South and West Yorkshire to Buckinghamshire, two areas of *bear-bind* — one in the west, bordering on the *convulvulus* area, and one in the south-east (parts of Kent and East Sussex) — and an area of *bell-bind* in Essex and south Suffolk. There are besides these a good many other local names — *morning glory, wandering-willy, robin-run-the-dike*, and so on — and, as with other plants, much folklore probably underlies such local names as *devil's-gut, -nightcap, -twine* in the north of England. The names for the couch-grass, goose-grass, charlock, colt's-foot (see fig. 5), cowslip, daisy and dandelion are also of interest from both dialectal and folklore points of view — as are doubtless others.

Children's words

A most interesting class of words are those used specifically by children. Some of these receive attention in Iona and Peter Opie's *The Lore and Language of Schoolchildren*, from which the examples here are taken. The expressions they recorded may have social distributions which cut across the regional ones, e.g. the same word for various notions might perhaps be found in public — but no other types of — schools in places as far apart as Manchester and Oxford. The words, too, seem to cross easily from one region to another, and even from one social class to another, resulting in a complex mixture of vocabulary.

Of the large number of words for **gaining possession** of something, *bags* is in general use and probably best-known, plus *bagsy* and *baggy mine*. The north-west (old West Riding,

Fig. 5. The *colt's-foot* or *foal's-foot*. Other names: *cleat(s), mugwort, batterdock, cankerweed, cock's-foot, coosil, dishilago*. Here reproduced from Leonard Fuch's herbal *De Historia Stirpium* (1542).

Lancashire, Cheshire) favours *ballow that* or *I ballows that, barley me that* and *I bollars* or *bollar me; ferry* also emerges in the old West Riding, *fogs* or *fog it* and *jigs it* in Manchester and elsewhere in the west midlands; *nab it, nag it, pike I* or *prior pike* are all west-midland terms too, and there are many others: note, e.g., *cogs* or *coggy* from Bury St Edmunds, *shigs* from Bishop Auckland.

Bags and many of the rest of these are also used for **getting first place,** the most distinctive terms being found in the north: from Stoke-on-Trent to Lincoln and from Lincoln northwards on the eastern side of the Pennines, the operative word — in various pronunciations — is *foggy* (*I'm foggy* means 'I have the right to be first'), while *laggy* means that the last place is wanted. *Ferry* prevails in the towns of the old West Riding — Bradford, Halifax, Huddersfield — the dividing line between *foggy* and *ferry* apparently running through Sheffield, Barnsley, Wakefield and Leeds. *Ferry* appears again in Furness and Cumbria, but *firsy* in Lancashire.

Perhaps the most crucial word in a schoolchild's lexicon is his **truce term,** used, sometimes with a sign such as crossing fingers or feet, to gain temporary relief from some boisterous activity, fighting or the like. The Opies' map of these words shows large areas of *skinch, kings* or *kings and crosses* in the east and of *barley* (adjoining) in the west, with *fainites* in the south-east and south-west, these large regions being penetrated by other, different, words: in the east (north to south) by *keys, croggie, screams, scores, croggies, scrogs,* with *boosey, scruces, exes* in East Anglia, and the large area of *fainites* in London and the Home Counties being pierced by *bruises, cruces* and *scruce;* in the west (north to south) by *keys, blobs, crogs, screase, nicks,* with *cree* and *cruce* on the south Wales border and *cruces, creases* in the Gloucestershire/Oxfordshire area. The south-west has *crease, bars(y), scrames* and *screams,* all occurring in a preponderantly *fainites* area, while the area between this and the south-eastern *fainites* area is filled in with *scribs* — *scrases, screens* and *creams, scrames* and *screams* also occurring. An especially interesting general point which emerged from the Opies' work was that urban children's usage may differ from that of the surrounding countryside; e.g. Lincoln city gave *screams,* while the rest of Lincolnshire was mainly *kings* or *kings and crosses.* There is, throughout the country, however, much mixing.

Spoil-sports and the like have a variety of names applied to them up and down the country, but a specially interesting one is shown on map 8: *mardy* is used in the first instance of a spoilt (i.e. 'marred') child, and then, more generally, of a peevish or moody child; thirdly of a 'soft' child or cry-baby.

To take a final example, the Opies found that **sweets** are referred to by the younger generation as *comforters, goodies, sucks* or *suckers* and *quenchers,* also as *candies* (in Cleethorpes), and always as *spice* in the old West Riding. They felt (this was in 1959) that *lollies* was also becoming a general term.

A comparison with information given by the elderly informants of the Leeds Survey of English Dialects round about the 1950s is revealing here. According to them, *comforters* and *quenchers* were unknown, *goodies* was a common term, though mainly found in Humberside, North Yorkshire and north Cumbria, *sucks* and *suckers* were midland terms, *candy* was given in Lincolnshire (though further south than the Opies found it), *spice* (locally *spahs*) in the old West Riding area, but *lollies* — with about a

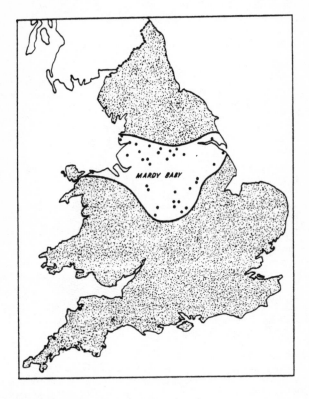

Map 8. The *mardy* area.

dozen examples — only in north Northamptonshire, Oxfordshire, west Buckinghamshire, east Wiltshire, north Hampshire and west Surrey. Has *lollies* spread from this area, or is its rise in popularity rather due to that of the 'lolly'-type sweet itself?

4. A look at history

To study English dialects without also studying their history deprives one of the perspective which tells us so much about their present condition. We shall now turn back to have a brief look at this.

The beginnings

The history of English begins when the Angles, Saxons and Jutes (also some Frisians) invaded Britain from the continental lowlands in the fifth century (although some were here much earlier), finding a population of Romanised Britons (Celts), and began to establish their kingdoms. Whether or not there were dialectal differences in their language even at the continental stage we do not know, but the Anglo-Saxon manuscripts which have come down to us from the eighth century onwards reveal several different *written* dialects (from which we can make inferences about the spoken language of the time), corresponding to the three Germanic tribes (above) mentioned by the Venerable Bede — a prime source — as having taken part in the invasions, namely:

1. Anglian, comprising (a) Northumbrian — found north of the river Humber as far as the Firth of Forth, and (b) Mercian — found between the Humber and the Thames.
2. West Saxon — found south of the Thames except for the region covered by —
3. Kentish — spoken by the Jutish colonists in Kent.

Of these, West Saxon is most fully represented in writing and was ultimately adopted as a standard literary dialect. These dialects form the basis of English, even as we know it today, and the roots of both present-day Standard English and the regional dialects are to be found here, although later history, as we shall see, has also had a large part to play. This 'Old English' period is usually regarded as lasting from the time of the first Anglo-Saxon writings (*c.* 700) up to about 1100 or 1150.

Celtic survival

During the Anglo-Saxon period groups of Britons remained, not only in western retreats, but scattered throughout England, their survival being evidenced by Anglo-Saxon law, river-names, and place-names such as Walcott, Walden and Walton which often contain the element *walh* 'foreigner, Welshman'. There may be evidence for the survival of Celtic dialects in the west of England until the ninth or tenth centuries, and in Cornwall the west of the county was Cornish-speaking until after 1500. As we have seen, some of the few Celtic words found in present-day English dialect — *bratt, brock,* also *ass* (ultimately from Latin) — derive from this early period.

The Scandinavians

Later in the Anglo-Saxon period another group of peoples began to have a much more decisive effect on both England and its language, namely the Scandinavians. The invasions of these barbarian peoples, mainly Norwegians and Danes, first struck England at the end of the eighth century. Later — by the second half of the ninth century — many of them began to settle more permanently, and by the eleventh century considerable integration of the two peoples — who during this period were mutually comprehensible in speech — had taken place.

The invaders came along two main routes: Danes (and some Swedes) sailed straight across the North Sea to Yorkshire and the east midlands; Norwegians arrived by way of the north of Scotland, settling in Shetland, Orkney, the Western Isles, the north of Ireland and the Isle of Man, from where they established permanent colonies in north-west England, especially in Cumbria and north Lancashire.

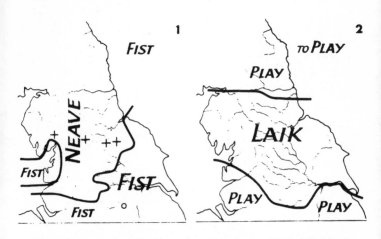

Map 9. Two more Scandinavian words: *neave* 'fist', *laik* 'play'.
Key (for 'fist'): + *fist,* o *neave.*

The only serious resistance to the Scandinavian attacks came from King Alfred, who defeated the Danes led by Guthrum in Wiltshire and then made peace with him in 878 by the Treaty of Wedmore. Under its terms England was divided, sovereignty over the region north and east of the old (Roman) Watling Street, stretching from London to Chester, being assigned to Guthrum, leaving London and the south and west to Alfred. A final period of attack, between 990 and 1016, resulted in the deposition of Ethelred the Unready and the succession of King Svein of Denmark, followed by his son, the great Canute, with whose reign Scandinavian attacks came to an end.

At first, Scandinavian words in English are few — only some eighty are to be detected in writings earlier than 1150, fairly common words like *egg* (verb), *husband, law, take* and *wrong*. However, by the thirteenth century many more appear in the extant documents, especially in those from the north and east midlands, doubtless having been adopted into spoken English in Anglo-Saxon times. Again, these are commonplace words like *both, dirt, ill, though* and *wing*.

Many Scandinavian words found their way only into northern and east-midland vernacular and survived there from Middle English times up to the nineteenth century or, in some cases, the present day. Many were mentioned in Chapter 2, but we may add the following: *blae-berry* 'bilberry' (ON *blá* 'blue' + OE *berige*), *drucken* 'drunken' (ON *drukkinn*), *feal* 'hide' (ON *fela*), *gaumless* 'stupid' (ON *gaumr* + OE *lǽs*), *grain* 'branch' (ON *greinn*), *lait* 'seek' (ON *leita*), *laik* 'play' (ON *leika*), *rawk* 'mist' (Old Scandinavian ·*raukr*), *skell(-boose)* 'partition in cow-house' (cf. ON *skilja* 'divide' + OE ·*bōs*). Neither should we forget that there may have been a certain phonetic influence.

The pattern of Scandinavian settlement — to the east of Watling Street and in the counties of the north-west (Lancashire and Cumbria) — suggests that the area of loan-words (see map 3) was originally somewhat more extensive than at present, their modern northern distribution being only a relic of this once larger area which, as place-name evidence tells us, once extended as far south as south Essex.

French influence

What we call the Middle English period is regarded as covering 1100 or 1150 to about 1450. About a hundred years before the beginning of this era the Norman Conquest brought about a decline in English literary production and also the demise of the West Saxon dialect as a standard literary dialect. English literature now came to be written in a wide variety of forms up and down the country and had also to contend with Anglo-Norman, a dialect of French developed on English soil as a second literary and official language. In the fourteenth century, however, English reappeared as the sole language of literature and of social and legal institutions, becoming increasingly used in literature and gradually being reinstated in all official spheres — courts, schools, universities and parliament.

Although — at least at the beginning — the French aristocracy had spoken only French, the English peasants meanwhile continuing with their native tongue, perhaps by the twelfth to thirteenth centuries many, if not most, nobles were bilingual, while there were also bilingual middle classes of both English and French, and this ultimately led to the extinction of French in England: once the conquerors had become merely a bilingual upper class, the way was open for the loss of the less useful 'upper' language and the reinstatement of the 'lower' (i.e. English).

While French was the dominant language, however, there had been much borrowing of French words into English, in both its spoken and written forms: words like *abbey, aunt, blanket, crown, jewel, stranger, tune, veal* — an estimated ten thousand or so by 1500, with more in later years. Some of these, in dialect, we had cause to mention earlier — *launder* 'gutter', *urchin* 'hedgehog', *tumble* etc 'farmcart', *court* 'farmyard', *mommet* 'scarecrow'. Neither must we forget the French element which emerged into the English dialect of west Cornwall via Cornish.

To these, however, we could add a great many more, e.g.: (Lincolnshire and Humberside) *cow-stable* (OE *cū* + OF *estable*); (Wiltshire) *vault* 'well, earth-closet' (OF *voute, volte*); (Cornwall) *planching* 'upstairs floor' (ultimately from Fr *planche* 'plank'); (south Devon) *causen* floor, 'flagged' floor (ONF *caucie* + *-en*); (northern and north-midland) *tunnel* 'funnel' (OF *tonel*); (south-western) *rummage* 'rubbish' (Fr *arrumage*); (south-western) *flask, flasket* 'clothes-basket' (OF *flasque, flasquet*) and *maund* 'feeding-basket' (for animals) (OF *mande*); (northern and midland) *bonny* 'pretty' (perhaps OF *bon*), and many more.

Other foreign contacts

France was England's chief foreign contact during and subsequent to the Middle Ages, but there was also intimate contact with the Low Countries from a very early date: the Flemish and Dutch had major roles in such English enterprises as weaving, sheep-rearing and the wool trade in Kent, market-gardening and fruit growing in the same county, engineering work in Dover harbour and the glass-making industry. There has also been a close connection between English and continental fishing communities, and further intercourse arose from sixteenth-century religious persecution on the Continent, when there was an influx of refugees to this country.

Loan-words from these sources are, although fewer than those from France, well-known in Standard English, e.g. *hop* (noun), *kit, skipper, slim,* perhaps *hoist* and *pack* and numerous others. And the dialects contain some further examples; to *spile, spill, splint* 'splinter' and *pad* 'path' one could add: (Devon) *brandis* 'gridiron' (cf. Du *brandijzer* 'branding-iron'); (widespread) *groop* 'drain in cow-house' (MDu *groepe*); (Northumberland and north Cumbrian) *keek* 'peep' (perhaps MDu *kieken* or LG *kîken*); (midlands and south-eastern) *snap* 'snack' (MDu or MLG *snappen*); (East Anglian) *stull* 'large piece of anything edible', e.g. bread (perhaps Frisian *stulle* 'piece, lump'); (south Devon, east and central Cornwall) *fitch* 'polecat' (early Du *fisse, visse, vitsche*). We may add, too, words from fishermen's dialect such as *lugger* (cf. Du *logger*) and *yawl* (apparently MLG *jolle* or Du *jol*), both names of small boats, *spill* 'shank of anchor' (apparently the same word as *spill* 'splinter'). Flemish influence may also be responsible for south-eastern **d** in *that, there, these,* etc (see page 27).

There has also been contact with Germany since the Middle Ages, especially in the field of mining, and some loan-words from this source are perhaps to be found, but contacts with Italy, Spain and Portugal have given us very few words which are specifically dialectal.

Standard English

As we have seen, in the fourteenth century English reasserted itself in social and literary spheres, and from this time English writings appear in numerous literary genres and a large number of different dialects — Kentish, Lincolnshire, Yorkshire, west-midland, Gloucestershire, London, Norfolk and a great many more. It is important to realise that at this time *all* English was dialectal: there was no one 'standard' form, spoken or written, but a large number of local ways of writing and speaking — 'local standards', as one might call them.

Out of this variety of local forms one in particular began to rise to pre-eminence, first in writing and then also in speech. This was an *upper-class* dialect developed in London in the fourteenth and fifteenth centuries mainly on the basis of the influential dialect of immigrants to the capital from the east midlands. From this time on, dialect characteristics began to disappear in both writings intended for the public and those of a private nature (diaries, letters, etc), while 'London' English became more and more the predominant form, being used for all purposes by educated men of every region. By the end of the seventeenth century most of the surviving variations in writing had gone, and there was more or less one norm.

In speech we have no direct evidence for a standard until much later, though we generally assume that a spoken standard arose not long after the written standard. But in 1589 the author of *The*

Map 10. Middle English dialects. The classification is necessarily a rough one pending further research.

Arte of English Poesie advised poets to adopt 'the usual speech of the Court, and that of London and the shires lying about London within sixty miles', and this is only one of a number of statements to the effect that educated, upper-class London and southern speech was by this time the model for those who wanted their speech to be of the 'best' sort. Provincialisms were ridiculed as barbaric by the seventeenth-century grammarians, and on the stage rustic speakers were given broad west-country dialects to emphasise their lowly status. As 'Standard English' rose in favour, so non-Standard types declined.

At first, however, early Standard English was reasonably free in its permission of variants in pronunciation and grammar, but the eighteenth century saw a movement towards uniformity in both. 'For pronunciation', stated Dr Johnson, 'the best general rule is to consider those as the most elegant speakers who deviate least from the written word.' Since this time, aided by the massive swing from rural to urban living which has taken place since the first half of the nineteenth century, the rise of public schools and later the BBC, variants in pronunciation (and indeed at all levels) have gradually disappeared and a Standard English based on the influential written standard has taken their place.

In the days before the growth of towns and their suburbs the patterning of English dialects was in the main geographical, but afterwards another patterning came more to the fore, namely a social one. In the towns, speech varieties classified themselves not on a geographical but on a social basis, in which the speech of non-dialect speakers emerged at the top of a scale of linguistic values, that of the speakers of the local form of speech at the bottom.

The fate of the regional dialects

In the countryside, meanwhile, the old rural dialects continued but were subject to a constant tendency towards modification in the direction of Standard English. In many areas, because of their comparative isolation, e.g. the Yorkshire Dales, rural Devon, this type of speech has been preserved remarkably well, although most dialect speakers are 'bi-dialectal' — they speak the local dialect within their own community but easily switch to Standard English for the benefit of outsiders or when away from their own home. Thomas Hardy captured this state of affairs well in *Tess of the d'Urbervilles* (1891), when he wrote:

> Mrs Durbeyfield habitually spoke the dialect; her daughter, who had passed the Sixth Standard in the National School under a London-trained mistress, spoke two languages: the dialect at home, more or less; ordinary English abroad and to persons of quality.

The present situation

In the countryside, then, much regional dialect remains, especially among the older people, although this is (as it has been for some hundreds of years) in a state of constant erosion by Standard English, especially as it is passed down to the new generations. Clearly, however, the extent to which the local dialect is eliminated differs from region to region and from family to family. In some areas it may be total, whereas in others the children and young people may possess and hand on the dialect in a reasonably good state of preservation. It is in the larger towns that we best see the social hierarchy referred to above, where there co-exist people with no dialect at all and people with the very marked dialect of the region, and in between a multiplicity of varieties — part regional, part non-regional. Recently there has emerged a new respect for regional dialect, but mainly in intellectual quarters. The reasons given for this are complex, but the chief of them — stated baldly — is that any type of speech is as adequate for communication as any other.

Dialect literature

People had been conscious of the existence of regional varieties of English from the fourteenth century onwards; they received attention from archaising poets like Edmund Spenser, from the antiquarians of the sixteenth and seventeenth centuries (Leland, Norden, Camden, Sir Thomas Browne) and from the grammarians of the sixteenth to eighteenth centuries. But from at least the seventeenth century on there were attempts to compile glossaries of local dialect and to write dialect poems, dialogues and other works, both to display the characteristic features of these moribund forms of speech and to preserve them from extinction. With the nineteenth century this was done on a more scientific and systematic basis, and dialect study was pursued — and has been ever since — with the aim of illuminating the history of the English language as a whole. Outstanding examples of such writers were the glossarists John Ray (1627-1705) and Francis Grose (c. 1731-91) — older glossaries are still of use in the investigation of the now obsolete vocabularies of different regions — the Yorkshireman George Meriton, who (c. 1683) wrote *A Yorkshire Dialogue,* in which he adapted the alphabet to express the sounds of the contemporary Yorkshire dialect, and the author of the *Exmoor Courtship* and *Exmoor Scolding.* Devonshire dialogues of just over three hundred lines each, first contributed to *The Gentleman's Magazine* in 1746.

During the nineteenth century dialect literature of this type flourished everywhere, but especially in the north of England, perhaps because, as Professor Brook says, it satisfied the needs of the new industrial communities then coming into existence. Here dialect writing still flourishes today, both under the auspices of the dialect societies and independently in the form of collections of dialect verse and contributions to journals.

5. Literary dialect

We must distinguish the dialect literature mentioned in the last chapter from 'literary dialect', i.e. the use of dialectal forms of speech for literary purposes. The latter has a long tradition in English literature, ranging from some 'northern' dialogue written by Chaucer for 'The Reeve's Tale' (end of the fourteenth century) to D. H. Lawrence's Nottinghamshire dialogues in *Lady Chatterley's Lover* (1928). This literary dialect consists of passages of verse or prose designed to give colour to an author's work by imitating characteristics of speech, regional and social. In addition, some writers, like William Barnes and Tennyson, have written complete poems in dialect. Here there is room for one representative sample only; let us consider the following passage:

> 'I said I was as good as anybody else in the world,
> din't I?' Arthur demanded. 'And I mean it. Do you
> think if I won the football pools I'd gi' yo' a penny on
> it? Or gi' anybody else owt? Not likely. I'd keep it all
> mysen, except for seeing my family right. I'd buy 'em
> a house and set 'em up for life, but anybody else
> could whistle for it. I've 'eard that blokes as win
> football pools get thousands o' beggin' letters, but yer
> know what I'd do if I got 'em? I'll tell yer what I'd do:
> I'd mek a bonfire on 'em.'

This is an extract from Alan Sillitoe's novel *Saturday Night and Sunday Morning*, published in 1958. In it the author aims to give a rough idea of the Nottingham dialect — note regional items like *yo'* 'you', *owt* 'anything', *mysen* 'myself', *mek* 'make', which are characteristic of the area. But by far the greater number of the features we can observe are not specially regional but merely non-standard. Note *din't, gi'*, 'a penny on it', 'a bonfire on 'em', *'em*, 'set 'em up' and 'whistle for it' (slang expressions), *'eard* (h- lost), *as* 'who', *o', beggin', yer*. These — showing loss of various consonants, substandard expressions and the like — are ubiquitous. There is thus a mixture, intending to give an impression both of local dialect and general substandard English, but without being incomprehensible. This type of dialect dialogue is a far cry from the efforts of Emily Bronte in *Wuthering Heights* and Bernard Shaw in *Captain Brassbound's Conversion*, who made serious attempts to reconstruct the sound-system of the dialects they were imitating, namely North Yorkshire and Cockney respectively.

Dialect on the stage, radio and television

Even from before the Elizabethan period there were attempts in plays to suggest regional dialect — the most notable being the use of a southern or south-western dialect to represent the common speech of the clod-hopping country yokel — although the playwrights tended not to give the dialect in any great detail, but left it to the performers to bring it alive from such indications as *cham* 'ich (i.e. I) am', *vell* 'fell', *zome* 'some'. As Shakespeare's Edgar says in *King Lear* (act IV, scene 6):

Chill not let go Zir, without vurther 'casion!

'I will not let go, sir, without further occasion' (i.e. cause).

In *Henry IV* and *Henry V*, Shakespeare's Mistress Quickly also provides an example of stage Cockney, a type which then disappears until the middle of the eighteenth century. Shaw's Drinkwater in *Captain Brassbound's Conversion* (1899) is a notable example of detailed Cockney speech for the stage. It is unusual, however, for modern playwrights to represent stage dialect in such great detail as Shaw did and more customary for any dialect speech required to be assumed by the actor himself.

In the twentieth century literary dialect has been extended to radio and television, and considerable effort is made nowadays when producing, for example, a play based on a novel by D. H. Lawrence to get the characters to speak an accurate regional and social dialect, without becoming unintelligible, not always easily achieved with the broader dialects.

In particular, there has been in recent years a growth of interest in the industrial north-east and its past and present social problems. This means that the dialect of the area, especially that of the working-class, has had to be reproduced on a large scale. Actors who are themselves natives of the area are frequently employed, and to good effect. One recent series of this type was impressive in marking the social differences between management (speaking 'modified regional dialect') and workers (with broad regional dialect).

There are a good many situation comedies whose characters need a dialect for humorous purposes. One of the most famous of recent years has been *Till Death us do Part*, centred round the voluble Alf Garnett and his family and set in east London. Here the dialect was completely genuine, with *bloody, nut, funny*, etc, pronounced as a near-**a** sound, 'glottalisation' of **t** (*wa'er* 'water', etc), the substitution of **th** by **f** and **dh** by **v** (*Smif* 'smith', *bruvver* 'brother'), and a proliferation of *ain't*s and other non-RSE grammatical forms.

To take another example, *The Liver Birds*, centred round two

Liverpool girls, also managed to capture 'modified Liverpudlian' in a genuinely convincing way, and other northern (Lancashire, Yorkshire) situation comedies are too numerous to mention. But again, all such series greatly benefit from the employment of actors and actresses who are themselves natives of the area concerned.

Individual English comedians frequently rely on either a Yorkshire/Lancashire voice or Cockney (but note Pam Ayres, with the reverted r and vowels of rural Buckinghamshire!). The comedian with an exaggerated upper-class voice is not as popular as he was, and regional dialect once more holds the stage. This perhaps coincides with a period in which RSE is not so much in the ascendant as a prestigious type of spoken English.

Some works containing literary dialect

G. Chaucer, 'The Reeve's Tale' in *The Canterbury Tales* (*c.* 1390; northern); early plays *Respublica* (*c.* 1553) and *Gammer Gurton's Needle* (*c.* 1560; both south-western); Edmund Spenser, *The Shepheardes Calendar* (1579; mainly northern and archaic); W. Shakespeare, *King Lear* (first printing 1608; act IV, some south-western); Ben Jonson, *A Tale of a Tub* (1596/7; south-western), *The Sad Shepherd* (first printing 1641; northern); works of the poets John Clare (1793-1864; Northamptonshire); Tennyson (1802-92; Lincolnshire dialect poems); William Barnes (1801-86; Dorset); Thomas Hardy (1840-1928; 'Wessex'); R. Kipling, *Barrack-Room Ballads* (1889-91; Cockney); novels of Hardy (above); George Eliot (1819-80; Warwickshire); E. Bronte (1818-48; North Yorkshire); C. Dickens (1812-70; Yorkshire, Lancashire, East Anglia); D. H. Lawrence (1885-1930; Nottinghamshire); and, more recently, the writers Thomas Armstrong, Phyllis Bentley, J. B. Priestley, John Braine, Alan Sillitoe, Stan Barstow (all northern). See also G. B. Shaw, *Captain Brassbound's Conversion* (1899; Cockney).

---

6. The study of dialect

Dialect study in England

Serious dialect study in England was prompted by the publication of German and French dialect work begun at the end of the last century. The English Dialect Society was founded in 1873, with the intention of collecting words from the regional dialects for an English dialect dictionary. These were published in numerous volumes, and all the material was later assembled, and a great deal more added, by Joseph Wright, Professor of Comparative Philology at Oxford, in the famous *English Dialect Dictionary* and *English Dialect Grammar* (1898-1905).

In the field of pronunciation, A. J. Ellis had by this time published a huge work *On Early English Pronunciation, Part V: The Existing Phonology of English Dialects* (1889).

In the present century the *Survey of English Dialects* (*SED;* 1962-71) was initiated by Harold Orton and Eugen Dieth at Leeds University in 1946 and, based on the answers to a lengthy questionnaire, provides a body of material relating to pronunciation, vocabulary and grammar from elderly people in

Fig. 6. Gunnerside 'Gunnar's pasture' (ON **Gunnarr** + **saetr**) in Swaledale. Dialect work for the Survey of English Dialects was carried out in the area.

313 (nearly all rural) localities in England. Together with the *Word Geography of England* (1974), the more recent *Linguistic Atlas of England* (1978), and *Word Maps* (1987) — based upon *SED* — it gives a unique description of traditional regional English dialect of the middle of the twentieth century. There are also tape-recordings from every locality, which are housed in the archives of the former Institute of Dialect and Folk Life Studies, School of English, University of Leeds.

Similar work, though based on different methods and emerging in a different form of presentation, is being done in the Survey of Anglo-Welsh Dialects at the University College of Swansea, the Linguistic Survey of Scotland (whose first two volumes are now in print in map form) at the University of Edinburgh, and surveys of Ulster dialects at Queen's University, Belfast, and the New University of Ulster at Coleraine.

Since 1964 the University of Sheffield's Centre for English Cultural Tradition and Language has collected material on all aspects of language and cultural traditions throughout the British Isles, as a basic resource for research. It has assembled a substantial body of data on regional and social dialects, slang, occupational vocabulary, proverbs and sayings, together with information on local and traditional customs and beliefs; the Centre also sponsors and directs many projects in the field of children's language and folklore. In particular, it is conducting an investigation of traditional verbal constraints used by adults in controlling the behaviour of children. Copies of the fieldwork data and tape-recordings of the English and Welsh Section of the *Atlas Linguarum Europae*, a survey of the vocabulary of 82 *SED* localities undertaken in the late 1970s, are deposited in the Centre's archives.

Traditional dialectology — 'linguistic geography' — has been mainly concerned with old regional dialect, in an attempt to shed light on the history of the English language by examining the old forms of word, but language has also a social dimension: as we have said, there is variation in speech between people of different classes as much as there is between people from different areas. Some scholars have, therefore, turned their attention to the sound systems found in urban dialects, to try to reveal this social linguistic 'stratification', since towns house large populations of different classes. This research, therefore, does not seek to elicit regional variation in the speech of one sector of the community only (i.e. the elderly section) but is concerned with variation between different sectors and classes as a result of social and economic causes. Many of these matters are discussed in *Studies in Linguistic Geography*, J. M. Kirk and others, Croom Helm, 1985.

Some guidelines for collecting dialect

Future research into dialects may well continue to concentrate on towns, since much work remains to be done on places as different as Birmingham and Canterbury, Harrogate and Northampton. This complex task, which needs training and experience, is on the whole best left to the experts, though there is no reason why vocabulary should not be collected in these places by serious amateurs.

There is more hope for the amateur in the field of traditional dialectology (including occupational dialect), and he might begin by joining one of the dialect societies to make contact with people of similar interests. A list is given at the end of this book.

Traditional dialect work is something like research into local history, which informed amateurs have undertaken for some time. But the *informed* is important! Mere odd-word collecting only results in a private museum of unconnected items, of limited interest. No dialect item is of value unless it is known *exactly where* it was picked up, *who* said it, and *when* it was collected.

Whatever aim one has, some reading about the history of the English language and the area (industry, etc) under scrutiny is always useful. If an area, look especially at the place-names with a reliable guide-book, and some reconnoitring, getting to know the terrain and the sort of place it is, number of inhabitants and so on, is indispensable. If you are looking for the oldest stratum of the dialect, go to the remotest villages and interview the oldest people there. If an industry or children's language is being investigated, you will probably go to a factory or school.

Informants

The important thing, however, is to find your informants (perhaps through the agency of friends and relatives, shopkeepers, local clergy, schoolteachers or librarians) — not casually sit around jotting down random words you may hear. You should find out your informant's name and address, age, place of birth and that of his parents, education, and how long he has spent in the district and in his occupation. Unless you are deliberately studying people of 'mixed pedigrees', it is important to select informants who have been natives of the district concerned since their early childhood, for speech habits begin early and someone who has lived up to the age of, say, eighteen in a nearby village might well have speech habits which really belong to a completely different dialect — perhaps on the other side of an important dialect boundary! So 'native residence' is crucial. If his family have been natives for hundreds of years, so much the better.

Informants should be willing to help and sound in wind and

limb. Deaf people and those with speech defects may prove unsuitable. People who do not speak dialect but only imitate it are *always* unsuitable — the information must be got at first hand, from genuine dialect speakers.

The interview should be conducted in a quiet place — preferably the informant's own home, where he will feel most at ease. Assume the role of pupil, with your informant as teacher: you need information — he can provide it.

Questions and responses

The answers you are seeking from your informant and the method of getting them will again depend on the sort of information you require. Sounds — phonology — need careful handling and without phonetic and philological training are better left to the experts. Vocabulary and grammar are more straightforward fields.

Dialect surveys have usually been carried out by questionnaire — a list of questions which, when put to an informant, will reveal by the answers received the essential components of his sound-system, vocabulary and grammar. You may use an existing questionnaire, like the well-known Dieth-Orton one, most carefully compiled for the Survey of English Dialects, or, perhaps better, you may compile your own, briefer version, specifically geared to what you are looking for. Pictures and diagrams (e.g. of parts of machinery — agricultural or industrial) are sometimes useful.

Questions should be either straightforward, like 'What do you call this' (putting your tongue out), or completing ones, like 'The place where you store your hay is called ...?', which the informant will then complete. But never say 'What do you call the hay-loft?' or the informant will simply say 'hay-loft' — your question has already suggested it to him. As a *very last* resort, however, you can say 'Would you ever call it a *tallet, shippon, mow-hay, linhay* (etc)?' Preferably record the answer in its context, e.g. 'We sometimes call that a ...?' and note also any 'incidental material' — remarks interspersed with the answers, e.g. 'That's slang' or 'My dad used to call it ...'

In place of the questionnaire method some investigators now prefer to make a longish tape-recording for future analysis. This is all right, except that you may not get all the information you require. Best of all, perhaps, if time permits, is questionnaire *plus* tape-recording. The latter could usefully include details of the informant's early life, methods of hedging or pig-killing, local anecdotes and so on. This should provide useful information additional to that elicited by the questionnaire.

Historical dialect

Investigating historical dialect is a more solitary occupation. Post-medieval documents such as account-books and inventories may reveal numerous local words (and suggest their pronunciations — but great care, and training, are needed here) for implements, tools and household goods, for even though dialects were starting to break down, local words are still quite frequent in such sources, and pursuing them is a fascinating and worthwhile occupation.

Institutions with active dialect interests

Centre for English Cultural Tradition and Language, University of Sheffield, Sheffield S10 2TN (see page 56; biennial journal: *Lore and Language*). Director: Professor J. D. A. Widdowson.

Centre for Research on the Languages of Scotland, University of Edinburgh. Co-directors: Professor W. Gillies, Professor C. Jones.

Department of Applied Linguistics and Language Centre, Birkbeck College, University of London, Malet Street, London WC1E 7HX.

Department of English, The Queen's University, Belfast BT7 1NN.

Department of English Language, School of English, University of Newcastle upon Tyne, Newcastle upon Tyne NE1 7RU.

Department of Irish Folklore, University College, Belfield, Dublin 4, Republic of Ireland.

Department of Linguistics, University College of North Wales, Bangor, Gwynedd LL57 2DG.

Devon Dialect Society, c/o Porch Cottage, East Budleigh, Budleigh Salterton, Devon EX9 7DU.

Devonshire Association for the Advancement of Science, Literature and Art, 7 The Close, Exeter, Devon EX5 4EY.

Edwin Waugh Society, c/o 128 Market Street, Whitworth, Rochdale, Lancashire OL12 8TG.

Federation of Old Cornwall Societies (biennial journal: *Old Cornwall*). Secretary: Miss J. Rendell MBE, Tremarsh, Launceston. Dialect recorder: Mrs S. Stevenson, 2 Upland Vean, Truro.

Lakeland Dialect Society (aims: to encourage dialect writing and foster interest in dialect at both academic and 'human' levels; annual *Journal*). Secretary: Mr I. Graham, Knox Croft, Thornby, Wigton, Cumbria CA7 0HQ.

Linguistic Survey of Scotland, The University, Edinburgh EH8 9YL.

Northumbriana, c/o Westgate House, Dogger Bank, Morpeth, Northumberland NE61 1RF.

Archives of the Survey of English Dialects, School of English, The University, Leeds (dialect dissertations, tape-recordings, etc). Curator: Professor T. A. Shippey.

Survey of Anglo-Welsh Dialects, Department of English, University College of Swansea, Singleton Park, Swansea SA2 8PP. Director: Dr D. Parry.

Tape-recorded Survey of Hiberno-English Speech, Ulster Folk and Transport Museum/Queen's University of Belfast. Director: Mr M. V. Barry.

Ulster Dialect Dictionary, Ulster Folk and Transport Museum. Editor: Dr C. Macafee.

Welsh Folk Museum, St Fagans, Cardiff CF5 6XB.

Wiltshire Folk Life Society, c/o Salisbury and South Wiltshire Museum, St Ann Street, Salisbury, Wiltshire SP1 2DT.

Yorkshire Dialect Society (aims: to encourage interest in and the study of Yorkshire dialect speech and literature and kindred subjects; annual *Transactions* and *Summer Bulletin*). Secretary: Mr S. Ellis, Farfields, Weeton Lane, Weeton, North Yorkshire LS17 0AN.

There may be other societies or organisations in your area. For further advice write to: The Centre for English Cultural Tradition and Language at its Sheffield address above.

Further reading

General works

The Archaeology of English. M. F. Wakelin. 1988.

Dialectology. J. K. Chambers and Peter Trudgill. Cambridge University Press, 1980.

Dialectology: An Introduction. W. N. Francis. Longman, 1983.

English Dialects. G. L. Brook. Deutsch, second edition 1965.

English Dialects: An Introduction. M. F. Wakelin, Athlone Press, second edition 1977.

A History of the English Language. A. C. Baugh and T. Cable. Routledge, third edition 1978.

Language Variation and Diversity. D. Graddol. Language in Use Block 1, Open University Press, 1981.

Language Variation and English. D. Stringer. Language and Learning Block 1, Open University Press, 1973.

Studies in Linguistic Geography. J. M. Kirk and others (editors).

Croom Helm, 1985.

The Study of Dialect. K. M. Petyt. Deutsch, 1980.

Varieties of English. G. L. Brook. Macmillan, 1973.

Varieties of English: Practice in Advanced Uses of English. H. L. B. Noody. Longman, 1970.

Variety in Contemporary English. W. R. O'Donnell and Loreto Todd. Allen & Unwin, 1980.

Regional and social dialect

Accents of English. J. C. Wells. Cambridge University Press, 1982. (Volume 2 on the British Isles.)

Broad Norfolk. Jonathan Mardle. Wensum Books, Norwich, 1973.

Cockney Dialect and Slang. Peter Wright. Batsford, 1981.

Cockney Past and Present. W. Matthews. Routledge, 1938.

Dialectology. J. K. Chambers and P. Trudgill. Cambridge University Press, 1980. (Quite theoretical.)

Dialects in the South-West of England: A Lexical Investigation. A. Fischer. Francke, Berne, 1976.

A Dictionary of the Sussex Dialect. W. D. Parish, revised H. Hall. Privately printed, 1957.

English Accents and Dialects. A. Hughes and P. Trudgill. Arnold, 1979. (Social and regional, but mainly urban. Accompanying tape.)

English Dialect Dictionary. Joseph Wright. Oxford University Press, 1898-1905. (Bibliography lists the older glossaries.)

English Dialect Grammar. J. Wright. Oxford University Press, 1905.

English Dialect Society publications (1873-96).

An Introduction to a Survey of Scottish Dialects. A. McIntosh. Nelson, 1952.

Journal of the Lakeland Dialect Society.

Journal of the Lancashire Dialect Society.

Language and History in Cornwall. M. F. Wakelin. Leicester University Press, 1975.

Language in the British Isles. Edited by P. Trudgill. Cambridge University Press, 1984. (Comprehensive survey.)

Lincolnshire Dialect. G. E. Campion. Richard Kay, Boston, 1976.

Linguistic Atlas of England. H. Orton, S. Sanderson and J. D. A. Widdowson. Croom Helm, 1978.

Linguistic Atlas of Scotland. J. Y. Mather and H. Speitel. Croom Helm, volumes I and II, 1975-7; volume III, 1986.

New Cambridge Bibliography of English Literature. Volume I, editor G. Watson. Cambridge University Press, 1974. (Columns 103-8 list glossaries, etc.)

A Northumberland and Durham Word Book. C. Geeson. Harold

Hill, Newcastle, 1969.

On Early English Pronunciation, Part V. A. J. Ellis. Early English Text Society, Extra Series, 1889.

Patterns in the Folk Speech of the British Isles. M. F. Wakelin and others. Athlone Press, 1972. (See especially paper on Scots-Irish boundary in Ulster.)

Phonological Atlas of the Northern Region. E. Kolb. Francke, Berne, 1966.

The Scottish-English Linguistic Border: Lexical Aspects. B. Glauser. Francke, Berne, 1974.

The Social Differentiation of English in Norwich. P. Trudgill. Cambridge University Press, 1974.

Sociolinguistic Patterns in British English. P. Trudgill and others. Edward Arnold, 1978. (Papers on Belfast, Glasgow, Edinburgh, Liverpool, Bradford, Newcastle, Reading and East Anglia.)

Staffordshire Dialect Words: A Historical Survey. David Wilson. Moorland Publishing Company, 1974.

A Structural Atlas of the English Dialects. P. M. Anderson. Croom Helm, 1987.

The Suffolk Dialect of the Twentieth Century. A. O. D. Claxton. Norman Adlard, Ipswich, 1954.

Survey of Anglo-Welsh Dialects. D. Parry. Lithograph (obtainable from the author), 1977-.

Survey of English Dialects. H. Orton and others. E. J. Arnold, 1962-71.

Transactions of the Yorkshire Dialect Society.

Ulster Dialects: An Introductory Symposium. Ulster Folk Museum, 1964.

Variation in an English Dialect. J. Cheshire. Cambridge University Press, 1982.

Varieties of English around the World: the South-west of England. M. F. Wakelin. Benjamin, Amsterdam, 1986. (Accompanying tape.)

Varieties of English around the World: Glasgow. C. Macafee. Benjamin, 1983. (Accompanying tape.)

West-Country Words and Ways. K. Phillips. David & Charles, 1976. (Cornwall.)

A Word-geography of Cornwall. David J. North and Adam Sharpe. Institute of Cornish Studies, 1980.

A Word Geography of England. H. Orton and N. Wright. Seminar Press, 1974.

Yorkshire Dialects. John Waddington-Feather. Dalesman Publishing Company, 1970.

Several reprints of older (nineteenth-century, early twentieth-century) works on the dialects of Buckinghamshire, Cheshire, Cumbria, Essex, Northamptonshire and Yorkshire (old West Riding) were published by E P Publishing, Wakefield.

Occupational and specialised dialects

A Dictionary of English Plant-Names. J. Britton and R. Holland. English Dialect Society, 1878-86.

A Dictionary of Rhyming Slang. J. Franklyn. Routledge, 1960.

A Dictionary of Sailors' Slang. W. Granville. Deutsch, 1962.

A Dictionary of the Underworld. E. Partridge. Routledge, third edition 1968.

A Glossary of Cornish Sea-Words. R. M. Nance, editor P. A. S. Pool. Federation of Old Cornwall Societies, Marazion, 1963.

A Glossary of Railwaymen's Talk. F. McKenna. History Workshop Pamphlets, 1970.

The Language of British Industry. Peter Wright. Macmillan, 1974.

The Lapwing in Britain. K. G. Spencer. A. Brown & Sons, London and Hull, 1953.

Lore and Language. Sheffield; see especially volume 2, number 1 (July 1974) on back-slang in Birmingham meat-trade.

The Lore and Language of Schoolchildren. I. and P. Opie. Oxford University Press, 1959.

Made in England. D. Hartley. Eyre Methuen, fourth edition 1974.

Provincial Names and Folk Lore of British Birds. C. Swainson. English Dialect Society, 1885.

The Terminology of Fishing. W. Elmer. Francke, Berne, 1973.

They Don't Speak Our Language. S. Rogers and others. Edward Arnold, 1976. (On language of children and adolescents.)

Traditional Country Craftsmen. J. Geraint Jenkins. Routledge, 1965.

Literary dialect

Authors who have used dialect for special purposes are listed on page 54. Note also the anthologies:

A Lancashire Anthology. May Yates. Hodder & Stoughton, 1923.

The White Rose Garland of Yorkshire Dialect Verse and Local and Folk-Lore Rhymes. Editors W. J. Halliday and A. S. Umpleby. Dent, 1949.

Further anthologies of verse published by the Yorkshire Dialect Society are available from the Librarian YDS, School of English, Leeds University.

Index